ANGER

CAC Publishing
Center for Action and Contemplation
cac.org

"*Oneing*" is an old English word that was used by Lady Julian of Norwich (1342–1416) to describe the encounter between God and the soul. The Center for Action and Contemplation proudly borrows the word to express the divine unity that stands behind all of the divisions, dichotomies, and dualisms in the world. We pray and publish with Jesus' words, "that all may be one" (John 17:21).

EDITOR:
Vanessa Guerin

ASSOCIATE EDITOR:
Shirin McArthur

PUBLISHER:
The Center for Action and Contemplation

ADVISORY BOARD:
David Benner
James Danaher
Ilia Delio, OSF
Sheryl Fullerton
Stephen Gaertner, OPraem
Ruth Patterson

Design and Composition by Nelson Kane

Cover: *Study of a Man Shouting* also known as *The Damned Soul* (detail), by Michelangelo Buonarroti, c. 1525–1534, Uffizi Gallery, Florence, Italy.

Oneing

VOLUME 6 NO. 1

EDITOR'S NOTE

Anger is an emotion that consumes mind and body —but sometimes anger is necessary for survival.

—Barbara Holmes

THIS EDITION OF *Oneing* looks at anger from as many perspectives as there are contributors to the journal, not to mention those sources referenced in the articles. The common threads that run through the issue include justifiable anger, shame and anger, grief and anger, and ways to manage anger—an emotion that can, indeed, consume mind and body unless, as Richard Rohr states in his introduction, "we . . . take the risk of *legitimate* attachment (fully feeling the emotion), learn its important message, and then have the presence and purpose to detach from that fascinating emotion after it has done its work."

There is much about which to be angry these days. Author-activist Brian McLaren, in his article, "Anger, Contemplation, and Action," makes no bones about the number of issues that stick in his craw—from "greedy corporate elites and their bought-and-paid-for politicians" to the insidiousness of "racism, America's original sin."

"Many spiritual traditions warn us against anger," writes Rev. Dr. Barbara Holmes in "Contemplating Anger," yet even "Jesus expressed righteous indignation when he encountered the unjust systems of religious and Roman authorities." In developing a theology of anger, Dr. Holmes suggests that "we all need a way to channel and reconcile our anger with our faith." A theology of anger is a spiritually healthy avenue—especially for people of color who continue to suffer from human-rights violations.

Hebrew Scripture scholar Walter Brueggemann, in his article on the Psalms, "The Costly Loss of Lament," seems to corroborate Holmes' theology of anger: "A God who must always be praised and never assaulted correlates with a development of 'False Self,' and an uncritical status quo. But a God who is available in assault correlates with the emergence of genuine self and the development of serious justice." Who is better able to hold the tension of our anger—even our rage—than the Source of all that is?

In "Arthritis of the Spirit," preacher Barbara Brown Taylor shares two stories to describe how anger can manifest physically when it's not addressed appropriately. The first story tells of a sales clerk whose angry responses were frightening to Barbara and whose angry emotion had disfigured the clerk, leaving its imprint on her very countenance. In the second, even more dramatic story, a woman tells of a time when her anger manifested in such a way that it transformed her into an unrecognizable creature—not only to herself, but to her children and her mother. One child responded afterward, "I was scared because I didn't know who you were."

"Often enough, of course, anger is disturbing. It unsettles the peace. It threatens the order of society. It raises our blood pressure. It troubles our dreams and keeps us awake at night," writes translator and poet Mark Burrows in his article, "In Defense of Anger." However, he continues, "at its core, such an anger, in its noble form, will arise as a creative passion," as it did for Martin Luther King, Jr., in his "Letter from a Birmingham Jail."

In her article, "The Second Sacred Gate," author and translator Mirabai Starr writes that, in the context of grief, "the power of our anger often correlates with the depth of our love." Mirabai has suffered the loss of family and friends and identifies the many forms that anger takes in the face of such grief, including anger toward God. Through this exploration, she recognizes that "grief is an opportunity to reclaim an authentic connection with Mystery."

One of the key threads throughout this edition of *Oneing* is the need for some type of contemplative practice. How else can we possibly endure our ongoing outrage at the mass killings, the abuse of political power, various social injustices, and the seeming disregard for the desecration of Mother Earth?

Finally, I invite you to recognize that the poems and articles have been placed in an order that allows them to build upon each other. I encourage you to read them consecutively, beginning with Richard Rohr's excellent introduction on the passion of anger and the consoling words of St. Teresa of Ávila—words that prepare you to enter into a possibly disturbing, yet certainly lively discussion among these contributors.

Vanessa Guerin,
Editor

CONTRIBUTORS

RICHARD ROHR is a Franciscan priest of the New Mexico Province and the Founding Director of the Center for Action and Contemplation in Albuquerque, New Mexico. An internationally recognized author and spiritual leader, Fr. Richard teaches primarily on incarnational mysticism, non-dual consciousness, and contemplation, with a particular emphasis on how these affect the social justice issues of our time. Along with many recorded conferences, he is the author of numerous books, including *The Divine Dance: The Trinity and Your Transformation* (with Mike Morrell) and *Just This*. To learn more about Fr. Richard Rohr and the CAC, visit https://cac.org/richard-rohr/richard-rohr-ofm/.

REV. DR. BARBARA A. HOLMES is a spiritual teacher and writer focused on African American spirituality, mysticism, cosmology, and culture. She is President Emerita of United Theological Seminary of the Twin Cities and served as Vice President of Academic Affairs and Dean of Memphis Theological Seminary. Dr. Holmes was called to ministry while working as a lawyer who specialized in civil litigation, corporate, and appellate practice. She was ordained in the Latter Rain Apostolic Holiness Church in Dallas, Texas. Dr. Holmes has worked with homeless missions, HIV/AIDS support groups, and international ministries in Kenya and Japan. The author of five books and numerous articles, her most recent publications include *Liberation and the Cosmos: Conversations with the Elders* and *Joy Unspeakable: Contemplative Practices of the Black Church*. Dr. Holmes will be presenting at CONSPIRE 2018, together with Richard Rohr, Barbara Brown Taylor, Brian McLaren, and Mirabai Starr. For conference dates and to register, visit cac.org.

REV. DR. ALLEN DWIGHT CALLAHAN is an ordained minister of the Progressive National Baptist Convention. He has taught and lectured at Harvard Divinity School, the Seminário Teológico Batista de Nordeste in Salvador, Brazil, and other distinguished institutions. Allen holds a BA in Religion from Princeton University and MA and PhD degrees from Harvard. He is the author of *Embassy of Onesimus: The Letter of Paul to Philemon*, *A Love Supreme: A History of the Johannine Tradition*, and *The Talking Book: African Americans and the Bible*, along with numerous scholarly articles. Allen has appeared as a commentator in documentaries featured on PBS, the History

Channel, and the Discovery Channel. To learn more about Allen Dwight Callahan, visit http://linkedin.com/in/allen-dwight-callahan-4a20a556 or contact him at allendcallahan@gmail.com.

WALTER BRUEGGEMANN, PhD, an ordained minister in the United Church of Christ, is one of the most influential Bible interpreters of our time. He is the author of over one hundred books and numerous scholarly articles. Dr. Brueggemann has served as faculty at Eden Theological Seminary and is William Marcellus McPheeters Professor Emeritus of Old Testament at Columbia Theological Seminary. Dr. Brueggemann's primary textual method is rhetorical criticism. His magnum opus, *Theology of the Old Testament*, is a rhetorical-critical look at the Old Testament through the lenses of "testimony, dispute, and advocacy." His best-known books include *The Prophetic Imagination* and *The Message of the Psalms*. His work inspires, energizes, and convicts, and he often makes time to interact personally with those to whom he speaks at large events. To learn more about Walter Brueggemann, visit http://www.walterbrueggemann.com/.

SARA JOLENA WOLCOTT, MDiv, practices eco-theology through healing, teaching, arting, speaking, and creating innovative, anti-colonial spiritual ecology solutions with religious and spiritual communities. Her background is in international sustainable development and she has worked internationally for over a decade in sustainable health, agriculture, and solutions to complex crises. A native of California, she is currently part of the Bronx River Watershed in New York State. Her online courses on "ReMembering for the Anthropocene Age" stem from her academic work at Union Theological Seminary in New York City. To learn more about Sara Jolena Wolcott, visit https://sarajwolcott.wixsite.com/sequoiasamanvaya.

SHIRIN MCARTHUR, MDiv, is a spiritual guide, writer, poet, and editor who lives in Arizona. She is a former CAC staff member and the Associate Editor of *Oneing*. She leads online and in-person retreats and her contemplative photography appears daily at https://www.instagram.com/shirinmcarthur/. Shirin's award-winning Prayerful Pondering blog, part of the Christian Century network, will soon transition from https://shirinmcarthur. wordpress.com to her forthcoming website: shirinmcarthur.com. Shirin McArthur may be reached at shirin@communicationclarified.com.

JOSH RADNOR is an actor, writer, filmmaker, director, and producer. He is best known for his leading role on CBS' series *How I Met Your Mother*. He also starred in the PBS Civil War drama, *Mercy Street*, and is currently on the NBC series, *Rise*. On the big screen, Josh has starred in *Afternoon Delight* and *Social Animals*. His directorial debut, *Happythankyoumoreplease*, won the Audience Award for Favorite US Drama at the 2010 Sundance Film Festival. Josh wrote, directed, produced, and starred in the critically acclaimed film, *Liberal Arts*. On stage, he has starred in on- and off-Broadway productions, including Richard Greenberg's *The Babylon Line*; *Sacred Valley*, which marked his debut as a playwright; Ayad Akhtar's Pulitzer Prize-winning *Disgraced*; and the stage adaptation of the 1967 film *The Graduate*. He recently teamed up with Ben Lee to form Radnor & Lee, an indie-folk duo. To learn more about Josh Radnor and access his newsy, wisdom-filled *Museletter*, visit http:// joshradnor.instapage.com/ and/or tag him @JoshRadnor.

Roshi Joan Halifax, PhD, is a Buddhist teacher, Zen priest, anthropologist, and pioneer in the field of end-of-life care. She is Founder, Abbot, and Head Teacher of Upaya Institute and Zen Center in Santa Fe, New Mexico. Roshi Joan works with dying people and teaches healthcare professionals and family caregivers. She is Director of the Project on Being with Dying and Founder of the Upaya Prison Project. Roshi Joan is also founder of the Nomads Clinic in Nepal. A Founding Teacher of the Zen Peacemaker Order and founder of Prajna Mountain Buddhist Order, her work and practice for more than four decades has focused on engaged Buddhism. Her numerous books include *The Human Encounter with Death* (with Stanislav Grof); *The Fruitful Darkness: A Journey Through Buddhist Practice and Tribal Wisdom*; and her forthcoming book, *Standing at the Edge: Finding Freedom Where Fear and Courage Meet*, to be released in May 2018. To learn more about Joan Halifax, visit https://www.upaya.org/about/roshi/.

Mark S. Burrows is a scholar of historical theology, translator, and poet. A longtime resident of New England, he currently teaches religion and literature at the Protestant University of Applied Sciences in Bochum, Germany. His most recent publications include *Meister Eckhart's Book of the Heart: Meditations for the Restless Soul*, with Jon M. Sweeney; a new translation of Rainer Maria Rilke's early poems, *Prayers of a Young Poet*; and a translation of the Iranian-German poet SAID's *99 Psalms*. A volume of his own poems, *The Chance of Home*, was published in February 2018. Mark is an oblate of Glastonbury Abbey in Hingham, Massachusetts, and is a member of the Bochumer Literaten, a circle of writers in Germany. To learn more about Mark Burrows, visit www.msburrows.com.

Rev. Barbara Brown Taylor is a *New York Times* best-selling author, teacher, theologian, and Episcopal priest. Her first memoir, *Leaving Church*, won an Author of the Year award from the Georgia Writers Association. Barbara's recent book, *Learning to Walk in the Dark*, was featured on the cover of *TIME*

Magazine. She has served on the faculties of Piedmont College, Columbia Theological Seminary, Candler School of Theology at Emory University, McAfee School of Theology at Mercer University, and the Certificate in Theological Studies program at Georgia's Lee Arrendale State Prison for Women. *TIME Magazine* included her on its 2014 list of 100 Most Influential People. She was named Georgia Woman of the Year in 2015 and received the Chautauqua Institution President's Medal in 2016. Barbara serves on the Board of Trustees for Mercer University and her fourteenth book, *Holy Envy*, is forthcoming in August 2018. Her work has been translated into five languages. Barbara will be presenting at CONSPIRE 2018, together with Richard Rohr, Barbara Holmes, Brian McLaren, and Mirabai Starr. For conference dates and to register, visit cac.org. To learn more about Barbara Brown Taylor, visit http://www.barbarabrowntaylor.com/.

Russ Hudson, one of the principal scholars and innovative thinkers in the Enneagram world today, is Executive Director of Enneagram Personality Types, Inc. and Co-Founder of The Enneagram Institute. He has been co-teaching the Enneagram Professional Training Programs since 1991 and is a Founding Director and former Vice-President of the International Enneagram Association. He is co-author of several books on the Enneagram, including *The Wisdom of the Enneagram: The Complete Guide to Psychological and Spiritual Growth for the Nine Personality Types.* To learn more about Russ Hudson and The Enneagram Institute, visit http://www.enneagraminstitute.com/.

Mirabai Starr lives in Taos, New Mexico, and was a professor of Philosophy and World Religions at the University of New Mexico–Taos for twenty years. She speaks internationally about the teachings of the mystics, contemplative practice, and interspiritual dialogue. A certified bereavement counselor, Mirabai helps mourners harness the transformational power of grief and loss. An author of creative nonfiction and translator of sacred literature, she has received critical acclaim for her revolutionary translations, including *Dark Night of the Soul* by St. John of the Cross and *The Interior Castle* by St. Teresa of Ávila. Her most recent book is *Caravan of No Despair: A Memoir of Loss and Transformation.* Mirabai will be presenting at CONSPIRE 2018, together with Richard Rohr, Barbara Brown Taylor, Barbara Holmes, and Brian McLaren. For conference dates and to register, visit cac.org. To learn more about Mirabai Starr, visit http://mirabaistarr.com/.

Brian D. McLaren is an author, speaker, activist, and public theologian. A former college English teacher and pastor, he is a passionate advocate for "a new kind of Christianity"—just, generous, and working with people of all faiths for the common good. Brian is an Auburn Senior Fellow and a leader in the Convergence Network's innovative training/mentoring program for pastors, church planters, and lay leaders. He works closely with the Center for Progressive Renewal, the Wild Goose Festival, and the Fair Food Program's Faith Working Group. In 2004, he was awarded a Doctor of Divinity Degree (honoris causa) from Carey Theological Seminary in Vancouver, Canada. In 2010, he received a second honorary doctorate from Virginia Theological Seminary. Author of over a dozen books, his recent titles include *The Great Spiritual Migration* and *Seeking Aliveness*. Brian will be presenting at CONSPIRE 2018, together with Richard Rohr, Barbara Brown Taylor, Barbara Holmes, and Mirabai Starr. For conference dates and to register, visit cac.org. To learn more about Brian McLaren, visit https:// brianmclaren.net/.

INTRODUCTION

Even if you are angry, do not sin because of it. Never let the sun set on your anger or you will give the devil a foothold.
—Ephesians 4:26

THIS OFT-MISSED LINE in the New Testament shows real insight and almost-modern psychological awareness. It is cleverly able to make a subtle distinction between having a feeling and being controlled by that feeling. Necessary and helpful emotions are very different than *personal identification* with those same emotions. Only the latter is seen as a problem, or a "foothold" for evil.

Unfortunately, it was a less helpful line in the Sermon on the Mount which tended to hold sway in most Christian thinking and has yielded some ongoing negative results. Jesus is quoted as saying, "Anyone who is angry with his brother will have to answer for it before the judge" (see Matthew 5:22). Linked with the prior verse, anger is seemingly presented as a moral equivalent to killing (see 5:21). This is a plausible interpretation from most translations. I believe this is Jesus' attempt to move morality and its judgment from external action to the interior and motivational level, and that is certainly an advance in consciousness. It took modern jurisprudence to recognize motive and intention as ethically significant.

However, I believe that Jesus is also saying that chosen and sustained anger can be its own kind of murder. It is a murdering of one's own soul, which often leads to justified killing for "godly" purposes. We cannot afford to be angry for long or the emotion *has us* instead of a self-possessed individual *having* a manageable emotion. We often give up our own inner freedom if we "let the sun go down on our anger" (see Ephesians 4:26).

Has murder, justified by righteous anger, not been the story line of much of history—and religious history in particular? Unfortunately, most Scripture translations do not make this clear. We ended up thinking that we could, and should, repress the emotion of anger—which never really works anyway, because it only comes out in indirect, unconscious, and unaccountable ways. Emotions do not just go away. *They must be felt, their honest message must be heard,* and *only then can we release ourselves from their fascination over us.* Yes, emotions, if you feed them, clearly have an addictive character to them. A few years ago, my best-selling CD was entitled *Emotional Sobriety.*

Emotions are necessary weather vanes, in great part *body-based,* to help us read situations quickly and perhaps in depth. But they are also learned and practiced neural responses, often *ego-based,* which have little to do with truth and much more to do with the story lines that we have learned and created. The ego loves to hold onto such emotions to justify itself, defend itself, and assert its power. There is nothing like an angry person to control an entire conversation!

Much of the work of emotional maturity is learning to distinguish between emotions that give us a helpful message about ourselves or the moment and emotions that are merely narcissistic reactions to the moment.

I dare to say that, until we have found our spiritual center and ground—outside and beyond ourselves—most of our emotional responses, including anger, are usually too self-referential to be helpful or truthful. They read the moment as if the "I," with its immediate needs and hurts, is a reference point for objective truth. It isn't. The small, defensive "I" cannot hold that space. Reality/God/Creation holds that space. Persisting in using the small self as an objective reference point will only create deeper problems in the long run; it will not solve them. Mere emotionalism just does not work. It needs to be balanced by reason, context, grace, and, frankly, free choice.

Seeing any emotion, even if it is negative, as a "sin" is not useful, because guilt and shame, or any sense that "God is upset" with us, usually only increases our negativity and fear—which causes us to close down all the more. In other words, our emotions become more complex, more conflicted, more repressed—and thus *less* honest "reflections" of reality. If an emotion does not help us read the situation better and more truthfully, we must let it go—for our own advantage.

Most of us are naturally good at *attachment,* but most of us also have very little training in *detachment* or letting go. Practicing detachment is one of the great tasks of any healthy spirituality, but, when carried to extreme, it almost took over in much of early Christianity, and that was not helpful. We must take the risk of *legitimate* attachment (fully feeling the emotion), learn its important message, and then have the presence and purpose to detach from that fascinating emotion after it has done its work. This is the gift and power of an emotionally mature person. We all like to work with and have friends like this.

Anger is good and very necessary to protect the appropriate boundaries of self and others. In men's work, we call it the "good warrior" archetype. On the other hand, anger becomes self-defeating and egocentric when it hangs around too long after we have received its message. Then it actually distorts the message. Sustained anger, or victimhood as an identity, is not a virtue, but a self-defeating vice. Indeed, in that sense, it deserves to be called a capital sin.

In my own experience, I find that the word *resentment* comes closer to naming the real danger and true capital sin here. Resentment is low-lying—we often call it "seething resentment"—and largely hidden in the unconscious, where the "I" does not need to take responsibility for it. At this level, it can persist for much of our life—and never look like a sin at all.

In this case, anger creates people who are triggered into negativity, although they never get overtly angry and thus avoid looking "sinful." This makes them even more unhelpful and disagreeable than obviously angry people. In that sense, conscious, visible, felt anger is a gift to consciousness and to community. We need it to know who we are and what boundaries must be defended—along with the depth of hurt and alienation with which we are dealing, in ourselves and in others.

I would much sooner live with a person who is free to get fully angry, and also free to move beyond that same anger, than with a negative person who is hard-wired with resentments and preexisting judgements. Their anger is so well-hidden and denied—even from themselves—that it never comes up for the fresh air of love, conversation, and needed forgiveness.

Richard Rohr

Eficacia De La Paciencia

Nada te turbe,
Nada te espante;
Todo se pasa,
Dios no se muda,
La Paciencia
Todo lo alcanza;
Quien a Dios tiene
Nada le falta.
Sólo Dios basta.

Efficacy of Patience

Let nothing trouble you;
Let nothing scare you,
All is fleeting,
God alone is unchanging.
Patience
Everything obtains.
Who possesses God,
Nothing wants.
God alone suffices.

—Santa Teresa de Ávila[1]

Contemplating Anger

By Barbara A. Holmes

Anger can actually be an expression of compassion, a willingness to uphold boundaries that are sacred, or stand up for someone who is being oppressed.

—Julie Peters

ANGER IS INTENSE. Often, there is a flash of heat and disorientation and the need to justify or retaliate. When I was a child, anger was my response to hurt feelings. When offended, I would lash out or run crying to my mom. In her arms, and with her reassurances, I could quell a heat of rage so intense that it threatened to overtake me. Anger is an emotion that consumes mind and body—but sometimes anger is necessary for survival.

I remember the anger of my baby sister, when she was only five years old and I was eight. As the eldest of my siblings, I decided that she could not play with us. I guess, from her perspective, my eight-year-old dictatorial mandates were too much to bear. She got angry, in only the way that a five-year-old can. She leaped on my back, wrapped her little legs around my waist, and bit me as hard as she could.

I was shocked by her anger and tenacity. The pain was secondary. There was not much that I could do: She would not let go, so I ran screaming through the house with my sister attached to my back, biting me. My mother tried to pry her loose but she held on tight. In retrospect, I don't blame her. I was quite the eight-year-old tyrant. When they finally pried her loose, she was completely oblivious to my parents' chastising or my tears. Instead, she was clapping and laughing, completely delighted with herself.

The next morning, just as I was waking up, she kissed my face. She was no longer angry, but I saw my tiny sibling in a different light and never excluded her again. This little one was not to be messed with. Her anger opened my eyes and made our relationship better. She was angry, and rightfully so. Her expression of anger was personal.

But anger is not limited to individuals. The anger expressed by marginalized communities is both personal and collective. In either context, righteous anger can be a catalyst for change.

A THEOLOGY OF ANGER

We should not be ashamed of anger. It's a very good and a very powerful thing that motivates us. But what we need to be ashamed of is the way we abuse it.

—Mahatma Gandhi

MANY SPIRITUAL TRADITIONS warn us against anger. We are told that anger provides fertile ground for seeds of discontent, anxiety, and potential harm to self and others. This is true. However, when systems of injustice inflict generational abuses upon people and communities because of their ethnicity, race, sexuality, and/or gender, anger as righteous indignation is appropriate, healthy, and necessary for survival.

Jesus expressed righteous indignation when he encountered the unjust systems of religious and Roman authorities, yet Christian theologies shy away from the integration of anger into their canons. How

Righteous anger can be
a catalyst for change.

can churches continue to ignore anger and still be relevant during this era when everyone is angry about everything? People of color are angry about police brutality, white supremacy, white privilege, and economic marginalization.

However, recent polls show that white men are the angriest group in the United States. They feel marginalized although they maintain dominance in the economic and social structures of our society. They feel threatened by immigration, diversity, and their declining percentage of the population. White women are angry about sexual harassment, glass ceilings in their workplaces, and some of the above. With all of this anger permeating society, I am suggesting that we all need a way to channel and reconcile our anger with our faith.

For people of color, we need this outlet to save our lives. We are dying from stress-related diseases and health disorders, with no way to interpret our anger through the lens of faith. Accordingly, I am proposing a theology of anger for communities under siege. A theology of anger assumes that anger as a response to injustice is spiritually healthy. My intent is to highlight three ways that anger can contribute to spiritual restoration.

First, a theology of anger invites us to wake up from the hypnotic influences of unrelenting oppression so that individuals and communities can shake off the shackles of denial, resignation, and nihilism. Cornel West defines nihilism as "the lived experience of coping with a life of horrifying meaninglessness, hopelessness, and (most important) lovelessness."[1] Second, a theology of anger can help us to construct healthy boundaries. Finally, the healthy expression of righteous anger can translate communal despair into compassionate action and justice-seeking. The Rev. Nelson Johnson reminds us that the dominant culture is also extremely traumatized by its own history of abuse. Many came to the west as bond and indentured servants. The question is whether or not we will recognize our wounds and the source of our anger so that we can heal ourselves and others, and awaken to our potential to embody the beloved community.

STAYING WOKE

CHARLOTTESVILLE WAS A wakeup call. When angry white men carry torches and march through town chanting Nazi slogans, it's time to wake up. It was a shock to be reminded yet again that the only nation that I claim as a space of belonging *isn't safe* for many of us. To make things worse, the forty-fifth president of the United States openly supported their racism by equating perpetrators and resistors. Perhaps we were naïve when we hoped that the election of one black president would heal our racial tensions.

In the midst of blatant communal oppression, anger wakes us up to the realization that change can only occur when we put our cell phones down and turn off our systems of entertainment. In my book *Race and the Cosmos: An Invitation to View the World Differently*, I offer the following observation,

> We weave gossamer webs of habit and familiarity that lull, sustain, and entangle us. But it is difficult to articulate creative solutions to intransigent problems while dazed.[2]

For people of color, anger wakes us up from our daze and desire to "fit in," no matter the cost. Writer Lawrence Ware discusses his own journey toward anger, a journey that ignited his love for the community. He says,

> I'd spent most of my life worrying if white folks would like me... wanting white employers to look favorably upon me. I spoke in a way meant to make white folks see me as intelligent. My whole life was spent centering whiteness.... I'd bought into the lie of white supremacy, and I had unwittingly arranged my life around the white gaze.[3]

He concludes,

> Yes, I am angry about the conditions of black, brown and red people in this country. Yes, I do think that the norms of oppression and marginalization need to change. I am radical, and I am angry. I am all these things because I unapologetically love my blackness and yours.[4]

During these times of deep division and unnecessary harm to the vulnerable, the anger of decent people everywhere is appropriate. Public and peaceful expression of that anger is a first step toward creating safe boundaries.

CREATING SACRED BOUNDARIES

WHEN THE HUMAN rights of people of color are violated, it is assumed that they will protest a little and forgive quickly. This grotesque ritual was evident after the murders of unarmed black teens by police and after the assassinations at Emmanuel AME Church of Charleston, South Carolina. One day after Dylann Roof killed the pastor and church members during Bible study, the families of the slain began offering forgiveness. They offered forgiveness without repentance, forgiveness without discussion of the underlying racism in this nation that fueled Roof's anger.

While we know that forgiveness is necessary, our communities and the nation need time to recognize the horror of these events. This is a communal contemplative moment, a time to sit with our anger and consider the path that we are on. Chaplain Joshua Lazard contends that rushing past anger to reconciliation short-circuits the opportunity to have necessary conversations about cause and effect and pathways toward resolution.

Why does society expect the harmed to forgive before the slain are even laid to rest? When my sister bit me, she was the one who kissed my face the next day to restore our relationship. Even at five years old, she knew that she'd hurt me, so she initiated the first steps toward forgiveness. As actor Jesse Williams noted during the 2016 BET awards, "The burden of the brutalized is not to comfort the bystander."[5] Is it the responsibility of the terrorized to forgive quickly,

For people of color, anger wakes us up from our daze and desire to "fit in," no matter the cost.

without any acknowledgement of wrongdoing or any attempt to heal the wounds? A theology of anger helps us to move forward when harm is done, but does not require instantaneous forgiveness. Instead, it invites us to create sacred boundaries so that we can express our righteous indignation as the first step toward a process of healing.

If we take a theology of anger seriously, first we come together, then we grieve together, then we consider where we are and where we are going. If there is opportunity, we engage in deep considerations of cause and effect, and we listen for the whispers of the Holy Spirit. Forgiveness is a process, not a quick antidote to hatred's slow-acting poison. Our health and wholeness require that we take off our masks of Christian piety and do the difficult work of acknowledging our anger, our vulnerability, and our pain. It is this contemplative work that moves us toward forgiveness, for when we recognize our own human frailty, we can more easily forgive the fragility and failings of others.

CHANNELING ANGER FOR SPIRITUAL WHOLENESS

This idea of having to explain why it's racial, while standing in our own blood is silly. It's racial because it doesn't happen to white people.
—Jesse Williams

COLLECTIVE AND PRODUCTIVE anger redirects our attention to the everyday survival and healing of our own community. As Williams notes, we cannot waste our energy explaining our anger when it should be obvious to all. Sometimes the anger of black folks is resistance but, more often, it is grief. During a demonstration in Minneapolis, Minnesota, after the police shot an unarmed black man, pastor Danny Givens of Above Every Name Ministry, publicly and peacefully challenged the Governor of Minnesota. He shouted into a microphone,

> Your people keep killing my people. You keep telling me that you are going to do something. I just want you to put some action on it, put some respect on our people's names.... This isn't black anger. This is black grief![6]

Pastor Givens wanted the governor to understand that grief, anger, and black joy are hard to separate. At funerals of young people slain by the police, expressions of black joy are common. This is not "joy" in the ordinary sense of the word. This is not the embodiment of the myth of the "happy Negro" dancing mindlessly. This is the communal performance of resistance and resilience through dancing and rhythmic movement. Funeral-car doors fly open, music is thumping, and the community dances its defiance of death and the society that produces it.

We are angry, we are grieving, we are performing black joy as a sign of our determination to survive. When my parents tried to pry my sister off my back, they were, in essence, letting her know that her behavior was inappropriate. My sister refused to respond to their commands because they had not intervened when I was excluding her. She was determined and so are we. She would not let go and neither will the most vulnerable among us. All we have is our tenacity and our refusal to passively submit to aggressions that threaten our existence. Until the killing of black and brown people stops, all peaceful methods of resistance are appropriate. Right now, our anger is our truth, and our anger is a sacred part of our humanity and our faith.   •

The Virtue of Anger

By Allen Dwight Callahan

B E YE ANGRY, and sin not" (see Ephesians 4:26) is one of the Bible's oft-quoted counsels on anger management.

Those who quote it are quoting a quote. The phrase is actually a quotation of Psalm 4:4, though in most Bibles it doesn't appear to be so because Psalm 4:4 is rendered differently in different versions:

> Tremble with fear and do not sin! Meditate as you lie in bed, and repent of your ways!
>
> (New English Version)

> Stand in awe, and sin not: commune with your own heart upon your bed, and be still.
>
> (King James Version)

> Be angry, and sin not: the things you say in your hearts, be sorry for them upon your beds.
>
> (Douay-Rheims Version)

Be careful not to sin, speak in your hearts, and on your beds keep silence.

(New Jerusalem Bible)

The verb at the beginning of the sentence in the original Hebrew of Psalm 4:4 means "to be agitated, to shake violently," that is, to do what people do when they are frightened or awestruck or angry. The verb could signify the "Trembling cold in ghastly fears" of William Blake's lover in his poem "Never Seek to Tell Thy Love,"[1] the "trembling with awe" of Dante's spirit in the *Divine Comedy*,[2] and "how anger trembles in the temples/in the chest, in the impatient muscles" in Mario Benedetti's poem "The First Glances."[3] The Hebrew verb here trembles with all these significations.

Elvis Presley once sang of being in love as leaving him "all shook up."[4] However, according to the ancient Hebrews, being in love doesn't do that. Being in love can make you work (see Genesis 29:18), it can make you sick (see Song of Solomon 5:8), and it can make you stupid (see Judges 16:15–17), but it doesn't make you shake violently. In ancient Hebrew, one could be shaken up due to fear, awe, or anger—the kind of emotion with which we wrestle in bed at night but can't "take lying down" even when we're lying down. It's the kind of emotion that not merely motivates us but agitates us—a James Bond-martini kind of emotion that leaves us shaken, not stirred.

Thus, the various translations of Psalm 4:4. The New English Version trembles with fear; the King James Version stands in awe; the Douay-Rheims Version is angry; and the New Jerusalem Bible, tacitly recognizing the hopeless ambiguity of the Hebrew, drops the bit about fear-or-awe-or-anger altogether and splits the difference with an exhortation to quiet mindfulness.

Faced with an outrage, anger is the

Ephesians 4:26, in the New Testament, is following the text of an ancient Greek translation of what we now call the Old Testament, called the Septuagint, which rendered the Hebrew of Psalm 4:4 with a Greek verb that could be roughly translated as "to get one's wrath on." Thus, the Septuagint, in effect, opted for the trembling anger of the Douay-Rheims Version published two millennia later. So, when the writer of Ephesians was Bible-dipping in the Old Testament for a verse on anger management, the Greek text of Psalm 4:4 fit the bill.

Perhaps this counsel has been lifted from one place and incongruously placed somewhere else by the writer of Ephesians much like a toothless man with someone else's dentures: The teeth are not really his teeth. They are not even real teeth, so there's bound to be some slippage and slurring of words. Maybe Psalm 4:4 wasn't really about anger; maybe it was about fear, or awe. Nevertheless, as it stands, Ephesians 4:26 is a biblical exhortation to manage neither our fear nor our awe, but our anger.

Well, sort of.

There are two imperatives in the opening phrase of Ephesians 4:26–two. One is a prohibition against sinning. The other is an exhortation—an exhortation to anger.

That's right: The Bible commands us to be angry.

"Be angry. That's an order."

And the command to be angry is especially timely these days, because we need to be encouraged to muster every bit of anger we can.

Now, you may object that we've already got more anger than we know what to do with right now, and, of course, you'd be right. There is indeed a surplus of anger out there. With increasing frequency and intensity, people are voicing their anger, venting their anger, even voting their anger.

But there's anger, and there's anger.

Yes, there's the anger of being cut off in the turn lane, of having a wait time that exceeds four minutes, of being berated in the comments on your post by a misanthropic troll, of being stuck with a politician you didn't vote for who is saying and doing things that aren't called for.

price we pay for paying attention.

Then there is the anger that leaves us shaken and shaking because a sacred trust is being treacherously broken; because those who have done no harm are being gratuitously harmed; because those who have too little now have even less, and those who already have much too much now have even more; because egregious wrongs are being perpetrated, and the perps don't even admit that the wrongs they're perpetrating are wrong.

What has happened—is happening now, here, and everywhere—is not merely a sin and a shame. It is an outrage, and outrage calls for rage, rage that ought to come out. Anger in such instances is not merely permissible. It is obligatory, imperative.

Thus, the imperative: "Be angry."

Faced with an outrage, anger is the price we pay for paying attention. It is the rage that ought to come out, because, when faced with an outrage, it is a sin *not* to be angry.

So, let us not sin. In these troubled, troubling days, let us be mad as hell about the outrages that rightly rob us of our sleep at night.

Anger is not an end of virtue. But, these days, anger is virtue's obligatory beginning. •

The Costly Loss of Lament

By Walter Brueggemann

STUDY OF THE LAMENT PSALMS has indicated their enormous theological significance for the faith and liturgy of Israel and for the subsequent use of the church. There is no doubt that the lament Psalms had an important function in the community of faith. I will explore the loss of life and faith incurred when the lament Psalms are no longer used for their specific social function.

I

CLAUS WESTERMANN has done the most to help our understanding of the Psalms and his work is surely normative for all other discussions.[1] He has shown that these Psalms move from plea to praise.[2] In that move the situation and/or attitude of the speaker is transformed, and God is mobilized for the sake of the speaker. The intervention of God in some way permits the move from plea to praise.[3]

The lament is resolved by and corresponds to the song of thanksgiving.[4] Indeed, the song of thanksgiving is the lament restated after the crisis has been dealt with. The lament characteristically ends in praise which is full and unfettered. Indeed, the proper setting of praise is as lament resolved. In a sense, doxology and praise are best understood only in response to God's salvific intervention which in turn is evoked by the lament.[5]

In these Psalms, Israel moves from *articulation* of hurt and anger to *submission* of them to God and finally *relinquishment*.[6] Functionally and experientially, the verbal articulation and the faithful submission to God are prerequisites for relinquishment. Only when there is such relinquishment can there be praise and acts of generosity.

[One] mode of interpretation has caused a sense of unreality about the laments, as though they are used as play-acting in some great national drama, rather than the serious experience of members of the community.

No doubt the language of the lament Psalms reflects a juridical concern. However, it is difficult to know how "realistically" to take the language. A Psalm like Psalm 109 suggests that the language is real-life.[7] The appeal for a judge is a real one. The prayer petition is a request that the actual juridical procedure should be handled in a certain way.

The laments are genuine pastoral activities. Personal laments function in a "Kleinkult" apart from the temple, where the personal life-cycle processes of birth and death are in crisis, in something like a house church or a base community in which members of the community enact a ritual of rehabilitation as an act of hope.

It is still the case that scholars have only walked around the edges of the theological significance of the lament Psalm. We have yet to ask what it means to have this form available.[8] What difference does it make to have faith that permits and requires this form of prayer? My answer is that it shifts the calculus and *redresses the redistribution of power* between the two parties, so that the petitionary party is taken seriously and the God who is addressed is newly engaged in the crisis in a way that puts God at risk. As the lesser petitionary party (the Psalm speaker) is legitimated, so the unmitigated supremacy of the greater party (God) is questioned, and God is made available to the petitioner. The speech of the petitioner is heard, valued, and transmitted as serious speech. Cultically, we may assume that such speech is taken seriously by God. Such a speech pattern and social usage keep all power relations under review and capable of redefinition.

The lament form thus concerns a redistribution of power. What happens when appreciation of the lament as a form of speech and faith is lost, as I think it is largely lost in contemporary usage? What happens when the speech forms that redress power distribution have been silenced and eliminated? The answer, I believe, is that a theological monopoly is re-enforced, docility and submissiveness are engendered, and the outcome in terms of social practice is to re-enforce and consolidate the political-economic monopoly of the status quo. That is, the removal of lament from life and liturgy is not disinterested and, I suggest, only partly unintentional. In the following I will explore two dimensions of loss and therefore two possible gains for the recovery of lament.

II

ONE LOSS THAT results from the absence of lament is the loss of *genuine covenant interaction* because the second party to the covenant (the petitioner) has become voiceless or has a voice that is permitted to speak only praise and doxology. Where lament is absent, covenant comes into being only as a celebration of joy and well-being. Or in political categories, the greater party is surrounded by subjects who are always "yes men and women." Since such a celebrative, consenting silence does not square with reality, covenant minus lament is finally a practice of denial, cover-up, and pretense, which sanctions social control.

There is important heuristic gain in relating this matter to the theory of personality development called "object-relations theory."[9] The child, if she is to develop ego-strength, must have initiative with the mother, must have experience of omnipotence, and this happens only if the mother is responsive to the child's gestures and does not take excessive initiative toward the child. The negative alternative is that the mother does not respond but takes initiative, and then the mother is experienced by the child as omnipotent:

The mother who is not good enough is not able to implement the infant's omnipotence and so she repeatedly fails to meet the infant gesture. Instead she substitutes her own gesture which is to be given compliance by the infant. This compliance on the part of the infant is the earliest stage of the False Self, and belongs to the mother's inability to sense her infant's needs.[10]

We can draw a suggestive analogy from this understanding of the infant/mother relationship for our study of the lament. Where there is lament, the believer is able to take initiative with God and so develop over against God the ego strength that is necessary for responsible faith. But where the capacity to initiate lament is absent, one is left only with praise and doxology. God then is omnipotent, always to be praised. The believer is nothing. The outcome is a "False Self," bad faith which is based in fear and guilt and lived out as resentful or self-deceptive works of righteousness. The absence of lament makes a religion of coercive obedience the only possibility.

I do not suggest that biblical faith be reduced to psychological categories, but I find this parallel suggestive. It suggests that the God who evokes and responds to lament is not omnipotent in any conventional sense or surrounded by docile reactors. Rather, this God is like a mother who dreams with this infant, that the infant may some day grow into a responsible, mature covenant partner who can enter into serious communion and conversation. In such a serious conversation and communion, there comes genuine obedience, which is not a contrived need to please, but a genuine, yielding commitment.

Where there is no lament through which the believer takes initiative, God is experienced like an omnipotent mother. What is left for the believer then is a false narcissism which keeps hoping for a centered self, but which lacks the ego strength for a real self to emerge.

III

THE SECOND LOSS caused by the absence of lament is the *stifling of the question of theodicy.* I do not refer to some esoteric question of God's coping with ontological evil. Rather, I mean the capacity to raise and legitimate questions of justice in terms of social goods, social access, and social power.[11] My sense is that, in the

Where there is no lament through which the believer takes initiative, God is experienced like an omnipotent mother.

Old Testament, Israel is more committed to questions of justice than to questions of God.[12] The lament partakes in something of a claim filed in court in order to ensure that the question of justice is formally articulated.

The lament Psalms, then, are a complaint which makes the shrill insistence:

1. Things are not right in the present arrangement.
2. They need not stay this way but can be changed.
3. The speaker will not accept them in this way, for it is intolerable.
4. It is God's obligation to change things.[13]

But the main point is the first. Life isn't right. It is now noticed and voiced that life is not as it was promised to be. The utterance of this awareness is an exceedingly dangerous moment at the throne. For the managers of the system—political, economic, religious, moral—there is always a hope that the troubled folks will not notice the dysfunction or that a tolerance of a certain degree of dysfunction can be accepted as normal and necessary, even if unpleasant. Lament occurs when the dysfunction reaches an unacceptable level, when the injustice is intolerable and change is insisted upon.

In regularly using the lament form, Israel kept the justice question visible and legitimate. It is the cry of Israel (Exodus 2:23–25) which mobilizes Yahweh to action that begins the history of Israel. The cry initiates history.[14] The cry mobilizes God in the arena of public life.

It is juridical action that rescues and judges. That is the nature of the function of lament in Israel.

Where lament is absent, *the normal mode of the theodicy question is forfeited.*[15] When the lament form is censured, justice questions cannot be asked and eventually become invisible and illegitimate. Instead we learn to settle for questions of "meaning,"[16] and we reduce the issues to resolutions of love. But the categories of meaning and love do not touch the public systemic questions about which biblical faith is relentlessly concerned. A community of faith which negates laments soon concludes that the hard issues of justice are improper questions to pose at the throne, because the throne seems to be only a place of praise. I believe it thus follows that if justice questions are improper questions at the throne, they soon appear to be improper questions in public places, in schools, in hospitals, with the government, and eventually even in the courts. Justice questions disappear into civility and docility.[17] The order of the day comes to seem absolute, beyond question, and we are left with only grim obedience and eventually despair. The point of access for serious change has been forfeited when the propriety of this speech form is denied.

IV

THE LAMENT MAKES an assertion about God: that this dangerous, available God matters in every dimension of life. Where God's dangerous availability is lost because we fail to carry on our part of the difficult conversation, where God's vulnerability and passion are removed from our speech, we are consigned to anxiety and despair and the world as we now have it becomes absolutized. Our understanding of faith is altered dramatically, depending on whether God is a dead cipher who cannot be addressed and is only the silent *guarantor* of the status quo, or whether God can be addressed in risky ways as the *transformer* of what has not yet appeared. A God who must always be praised and never assaulted correlates with a development of "False Self," and an uncritical status quo. But a God who is available in assault correlates with the emergence of genuine self and the development of serious justice.

V

FINALLY, I CONCLUDE with some brief comments on Psalm 39, to see how these claims are worked out in a specific text. Psalm 39 is a lament which makes petition to Yahweh. The speaker announces his long-standing intention to keep silent (verses 1–3a). But the practice of restraint only contributed to the trouble. In verse 3b, finally there is speech, because the submissive silence was inadequate. In verse 4, the speaker names Yahweh for the first time. In that moment of speech of bold address, things already begin to change. The cause of trouble has now become an open question in the relationship. The speaker resolves no longer to be dumb in the face of wickedness. That resolve creates new possibilities.

The mood changes abruptly in verse 7, in which God is addressed for the second time. The crucial rhetorical move is *we'attâ*, "and now."[18] A major turn is marked as the speech moves from meditation to active, insistent hope.

The focus on Yahweh is an insistence that things need not and will not stay as they are. This is followed in verse 8 by a powerful imperative, *nṣl*, "snatch" or "deliver." In verse 9, the petition grows bolder because now the speaker is able to say *"You have done it."* The accusation is a form of active hope. Then in verse 12, the third reference to Yahweh is again a vigorous imperative:

> Hear my prayer, Yahweh
> to my cry give ear,
> at my tears do not be silent
> for I am a sojourner with you.

The speech which has ended the silence is a strong urging to Yahweh. As the speaker has refused silence, now he petitions Yahweh also to break the silence (verse 12). The speech of the petitioner seeks to evoke the speech and intervention of Yahweh.

The Psalm ends with the terse *'ēnenî*, "I will not be." The urging is that God should act before the speaker ceases to be, as a result of a process of social nullification. Whether the speaker ceases to be depends on Yahweh's direct intervention, in the face of powerful forces which practice nullification.

I submit that this Psalm makes contact with both points I have argued. On the one hand, the speaker moves from silence to speech,[19] to a series of bold imperatives, and in verse 9 to a clarification which may be read as an indictment of God: "You have done it." The Psalm evidences courage and ego strength before Yahweh which permits an act of hope, expectant imperatives, and an insistence that things be changed before it is too late.[20] The insistence addressed to Yahweh is matched by a sense of urgency about the threat of not-being. I take this threat to be social and worked through the social system.

On the other hand, the justice questions are raised. They are raised as early as verse 1 with reference to the wicked (raša').[21] The reference to "sojourner" in verse 12 suggests that the question concerns social power and social location which has left the speaker exposed, vulnerable and without security (except for Yahweh).[22] Yahweh is reminded that he is responsible for such a sojourner and is called to accountability on their behalf, because "*I am a sojourner with you.*"

On both grounds of *ego-assertion* and *public justice*, Psalm 39 causes a change in heaven with a derivative resolution of social systems on earth. Where the cry is not voiced, heaven is not moved and history is not initiated. And then the end is hopelessness. Where the cry is seriously voiced, heaven may answer and earth may have a new chance. The new resolve in heaven and the new possibility on earth depend on the initiation of protest.

VI

IT MAKES ONE wonder about the price of our civility, that this chance in our faith has largely been lost because the lament Psalms have dropped out of the functioning canon. In that loss we may unwittingly endorse the False Self that can take no initiative toward an omnipotent God. We may also unwittingly endorse unjust systems about which no questions can properly be raised. In the absence of lament, we may be engaged in uncritical history-stifling praise. If we care about authenticity and justice, the recovery of these texts is urgent.   •

"The Costly Loss of Lament" by Walter Brueggemann is an abridged version of the article which was originally published in 1986 in Journal for the Study of the Old Testament. *Reprinted with permission of the author.*

Learning of Fire:

An Interview with Sara Jolena Wolcott

By Shirin McArthur

Sara Jolena Wolcott practices eco-theology through healing, teaching, arting, speaking, and creating innovative, anti-colonial spiritual ecology solutions with religious and spiritual communities. Her background is in international sustainable development.

Shirin McArthur: How would you define anger?

Sara Jolena Wolcott: Increasingly, I see anger as being like fire. Fire is necessary for life. I don't mean to say that anger is necessary for life, so perhaps it is better to say that anger is a part of the larger fire in our lives. Anger is an important emotion; it is part of the flight-or-fight response that is core to how humans respond to danger. As such, it has a valuable role to play in our lives. It is important to feel fire's heat, but fire can burn out of control. The trick with anger is to let it inform us, maybe even to let it warm us if we have become too cold with indifference or apathy, but not to let the fire control or consume us.

Ultimately, we want our lives to be guided: illuminated, warmed, comforted, provoked by our deep love affair with the Divine. That love, as so many mystics remind us, can also be like an all-consuming fire. So love, not anger, needs to be the ultimate guide. Sometimes anger can point us to love.

Shirin: How does anger show up in your work?

Sara: In my own work, anger has been a clarifying fire. It has helped to burn through my own personal bullshit. Anger has shown me what really matters. Getting in touch with my anger about the pollution of our soil, water, and air helps to keep me engaged with climate-change issues when all sorts of other things—disappointment, inconvenience, lack of money, practical challenges, fears, etc.—prompt me to want to give up or do something else.

Of course, anger plays a notorious role for protestors of all kinds. A Lutheran bishop recently reminded me that Martin Luther (1483–1546) had a lot of anger; that is part of what compelled him to act as he did. Researchers point out that anger arises from a sense of something being "wrong"—and understanding that it could change. Anger can help us to get unstuck and lead us into action, which is desperately needed for us to create the world we want to live in. It is very easy to rest in a place where we cannot blossom into what God wants us to be, either as individuals or communities. Anger can help us move.

Anger has helped me to leave harmful relationships or work situations; I have seen it do the same for others as well. But there have also been times when my own anger has threatened the work I was doing, such as when I got angry at a teammate and was not able to communicate effectively. The key issue was not that I experienced anger, but how I responded to the anger, as a result of not being able to think clearly.

It is also important to keep in mind the difference between anger that comes from a place of our own ego vs. anger that comes from a place of seeing and seeking to right injustice.

Shirin: Can you say more about the spiritual dimensions of anger and justice?

Sara: I have sympathy with those spiritual leaders who say we should strive to get rid of anger, or at least to not act in anger. Yet the classic example of anger and spiritual teachers, at least within Christianity, is when Jesus overthrew the moneychangers' tables (see

Matthew 21:12–13). If the son of God can do this, we get the sense that it is fully acceptable to be righteously angry at systemic injustice that harms the poor and the vulnerable.

However, in the end, I don't think Jesus' passion or his death were lived through in anger—certainly his resurrection did not arise from a place of anger. So, what does that tell us? Anger can inform us and sometimes guide us, but anger is not the ultimate, final word; love is. Love is bigger than anger. Love still overtakes the divisions and fractions. I think there is room for anger in love. It is in God's holy fires that these emotions can be used well.

A key part of the spiritual path is how we work with—note I do not say avoid or squelch or ignore—anger. Anger that leads to right action might well be a prerequisite for the spiritual life in our age: "If you aren't outraged, you aren't paying attention." Not paying attention is not going to help you spiritually *at all*.

It takes tremendous spiritual discipline to let your anger come out appropriately—and to learn to see what "appropriate" is. Protest is often appropriate. So are creating new institutions and the necessary social norms that allow them to thrive.

We are in desperate need of new institutions that can be attuned to watersheds; that is a huge task, involving everything from engaging with local planning departments to working across state lines. If you think you are the only one who is suffering, or for whom the current system is not working (frequently causing frustration, which is a variation of anger), then you are unlikely to form the new networks and structures that will enable all of us to live together better. Often, in the work of climate change—of transforming institutions and individuals to live in the Anthropocene Age—I wish people would pay more attention to their anger and not try to shut it away. But we have become afraid of our anger. This doesn't help. Neither do we want to be consumed by it.

In all of this, we need guidance. I have been helped immensely by knowing practically spiritual people—ordinary saints, if you will—who can work well with anger. This includes people who work with and within complex organizations that seem bent toward continuing practices that actually harm people and planet. I encourage people to find those individuals who work well with anger and learn from them. Once you start asking, more teachers will come to you.

Shirin: Beyond learning how to control anger, what have you learned from these ordinary saints?

Anger that leads to right action might well be a prerequisite for the spiritual life in our age.

Sara: Oh, so much. I've learned a lot about developing practices of self-soothing. I'm not, again, saying we should ignore emotions such as anger. But when anger consumes us, it can be immensely self-destructive. I'm referring to anger that can turn into depression or long-term resentment. I've known many people who have a lot to offer but who are overtaken by resentment. Our world is broken. It is for us to be recognizing that which is beautiful and using our creative capacities for healing.

Then there is grief: I find that grief often underlies anger. Finding ways to recharge, self-soothe, and not become caught up in someone else's story or situation is critical. For some, taking up sports such as kick-boxing, martial arts, or other "violent" activities can be very help- ful. I think this is particularly true for people who work as caretakers and healers. It is so easy to internalize so much "shtuff" from your clients or patients, and giving yourself a very safe space where you can let it all out can make sure it doesn't come out when you are seeking to be a calm and collected presence for other people. It helps to have a lot of physical, as well as spiritual, core strength.

In addition to primarily working with spiritual-cultural creative responses and innovations for climate change, I've also worked in a jail as a chaplain. During that time, I witnessed many things to be angry about. The whole system of incarceration is so racist and broken, and often exacerbates preexisting wounds and vulnerabilities. In prison, anger is a hard emotion. You can't do much about where you are when you are there—be you the inmate or the officer or even the chaplain. On the one hand, you have to accept your current context; on the other hand, you have to keep "fighting," to carry on and not define yourself by your context.

Many people became defined by their anger. Some people were cruel but many were not, and they were always inspiring. Some of my teachers were the inmates themselves: Learning how they took joy and found meaning in very small things, and often learned a certain amount of detachment from their context, showed me ways of being engaged but also detached. Sometimes I would meet an amazing soul who really shone, who was not so bogged down by the grayness, the depression, and the anger all around her. These people walked their lives with kindness and strength. Anger did not define them; neither did their context.

Shirin: You're a Quaker. Quakers are known for being peacemakers. How do you reconcile your appropriate use of anger with this stereotype—or is it a stereotype?

Sara: The stereotype is that pacifism means you are removed from emotions like anger. That is wrong. If you link pacifism with inactivity, you are getting into navel-gazing inertia and self-indulgence. We need action, and we need the wisdom to guide it. Jesus, whom I see as a profound pacifist, was not inactive.

To work for peace is to take action. Peace requires even more action than does fighting because we must actively work against the entrenched tendencies toward aggressive, physical conflict. It takes almost no effort to pick a fight with someone: Just say a few casual words and, if the other person is already upset, anxious, or wanting to defend their social position, then you've got a fight on your hands. In the wrong context, that scuffle can lead to a massive war—take World War I, for example, which started out with something very minor and quickly escalated into a four-year international conflict that destroyed millions of human and non-human lives.

It takes significantly more maturity and right action to actually deal with the underlying conflicts without violence. Consistent spiritual practices support the spiritual depth needed to reach the wholeness and love beyond conflict. My best understanding as to why war is not obsolete is a basic lack of spiritual maturity among diverse peoples. After all, no one really wins a war. That's easy to see with children. If two children come home from a fight, both will be dirty, and possibly both will be broken and hurt. So, who really won? The great preacher, pastor, and mystical activist Howard Thurman (1899–1981) had this insight when he was a child and it is part of why he became a lifelong peace-bringer. Pacifism does not result from having no anger. It results from learning to be adults who value our own souls and who do not want to tarnish ourselves by killing another human being.

I do not think Quakers are any better at not being angry than any other religious group. Sometimes I think we are too passive-aggressive, and actually not good at talking about what is really going on. This leads to people seething, or not taking risks, or feeling insecure about their religious journey and identity. But, mostly, we understand the futility of outward forms of violence. We choose to envision the possibility that the truth of the soul—what Mahatma Gandhi (1869–1948) so beautifully referred to as *satyagraha*—is powerful enough and strong enough that we do not need to resort to brute force to resolve conflict. We remember that we are created from and with love. Love can hold within its embrace hatred and anger. We consistently seek ways to do away with the seeds of war. If we don't plant seeds of peace, the fruit won't blossom. It is quite simple.   •

Saluting the Divinity in You

By Josh Radnor

THERE ARE TWO Hollywoods. The first is a densely populated neighborhood on the east side of Los Angeles, which happens to be where I live. The second is the mythic center of the American film and television industry, which happens to be where I work.

I've always loved living in the first Hollywood and felt somewhat conflicted about working in the second. I'm from Ohio and trained to be an actor in New York, where living and working in Los Angeles was viewed, at best, as a necessary evil. There existed some widespread belief among New York actors—at least in the late 1990s—that Los Angeles was unserious and artistically compromising. I reflexively bought into that.

Then I actually went to Los Angeles and was startled to find I loved it. Who knew that one could spend an entire February not in the grips of crippling seasonal affective disorder?

Hollywood is too vast and multivalent to be reduced to cliché. The film and television industry isn't just actors and directors and producers. It's hairstylists and costume designers and grips and gaffers and sound technicians and camera operators and teamsters. It's actually a lot like many other industries, full of wonderful, wise, talented people and, of course, other, less savory characters.

The dross of Hollywood has been grabbing a lot of headlines lately. A very particular kind of darkness is being exposed, and that's a good thing. Part of the reason the current wave of sexual harassment/assault revelations began in Hollywood is that the world tends to pay attention to Hollywood. It's like life, just amplified. I've always taken this aspect of the business very seriously. People are watching, and what you do behind the cameras can be as consequential as what you do in front.

So, what's going on? What has created this culture of groping, leering, harassing, entitled, bullying men?

There's a part of me that thinks, "It's not hard to *not* be horrible. It's not hard to *not* rape, grab, grope, ogle, harass, squeeze, manipulate, demean, belittle, or bully women. It's simply *not*." I hate this whole notion that men just can't help themselves—i.e. the all-too-common pre-September 2017 excuse that greeted complaints: "Oh, that's just John being John."

I want to stop the analysis there, at: "Men, knock it off. Be decent." But that feels like a dodge, and obviously more consequential action is needed than a stern rap on the knuckles. Something massive and deeply broken is being brought to light—in Hollywood and beyond—and while it may be painful to look at the roots and shadows of it, this process feels essential and long overdue.

I think it's important to remember that no one behaves abominably in a vacuum. These men are a product of systems and cultural forces, as we all are. The problem, after all, is not a few bad apples. We must look at the whole tree.

If we're going to talk about men, we have to talk about boys—specifically, how we raise them. The cultural message to boys is clear: *Be tough, be a man, don't cry, don't be a girl....* I did not grow up in a cold, militaristic, overly masculinized household, but still: From a very young age, I knew that I didn't want to cry publicly, I didn't want to be thought of as "soft" or "feminine," I longed to be less sensitive and emotional. Fortunately, I found my way to the theater, which served as a healthy repository for all that aimless sensitivity.

Boys are systematically trained to hate that which is considered *feminine*—vulnerability, patience, receptivity, compassion, selflessness, to name a few—and to deny, denigrate, and destroy these qualities which exist naturally within them (and are vital in making one fully human). That which is loathed internally is surely going to be loathed externally, exemplified in the Jungian maxim: *That which isn't claimed is projected.* Thus, you have this powder keg of male hostility toward women (I'm framing this largely from a heterosexual point of view, but the damage extends in all directions).

Misogyny is absolutely baked into the way we raise children.

The damage begins early. Then—in a kind of sick cosmic joke—our bodies mature long before the rest of us does. Puberty is a trauma from which no human being escapes. (A friend told me he'd heard someone describe puberty as "a Ferrari engine being placed inside a go-cart.") Young men—who really know very little about the world—are taught that the height of human experience is sexual conquest and gratification. We're told in countless ways that this is *the point* of being a man on the earth.

In his essential writings on men,[1] Richard Rohr notes that male initiation rites in almost every culture throughout the world involve some form of forced powerlessness. The idea behind this is that if young boys are not acquainted with vulnerability and powerlessness, when they get some power as adults, they will surely abuse it.

We don't train our young men in this manner. Power, wealth, and fame thrust upon uninitiated (i.e. unconscious) adult men is then a recipe for disaster.

∾

IN HIS BOOK *Carpe Jugulum,* Terry Pratchett has a character define sin thusly: "Sin, young man, is when you treat people like things."[2]

I'm entirely on board with this. The gravest form of disrespect is to reduce someone to an object at the mercy of one's whims and predilections. We're seeing the consequences of this everywhere these days: People are being *objectified.* (Salma Hayek, in her recent piece in *The New York Times,* wrote of Harvey Weinstein: "In his eyes, I was not an artist. I wasn't even a person. I was a thing: not a nobody, but a body."[3])

An object is lifeless and inert. We have no inherent relationships with objects because we deny them agency and interiority. They are wholly *other*; their pain has little to no effect on us. A subject, on the other hand, is vivid, complicated, dimensional, imbued with the light of consciousness.

I believe mass shooters—in their horribly deranged calculus—are gunning down objects, not subjects. People must be reduced, robbed of soul, for true harm to be unleashed. Witness every genocidal regime in history and the words they very intentionally assign to their eventual victims: *vermin, bugs, cockroaches*; something foul and less-than-human that must be extinguished.

Objectification is a kind of inverse idolatry, the debasement and degradation of that which is sacred. The transition we're being asked to make—seeing the other as subject rather than object—is a restoration and reclamation of the sacred.

One of my favorite quotes from Iris Murdoch illustrates this beautifully: "*Love is the extremely difficult realization that something other than oneself is real.*"[4]

This is the root of the issue of representation in Hollywood: People of all genders, ages, nationalities, sexual orientations, races, and religions are demanding to be subjects rather than objects, the complicated centers of stories rather than one-dimensional props. People rightly wish to see themselves, in their full humanity, represented on screen in the stories we tell ourselves about ourselves.

THERE IS A WORD I hope will be liberated from the clutches of cliché: *Namaste*. The word tends to conjure up images of new-agers bowing to each other after yoga classes, but, like with all clichés, there's a big beating heart to the thing in its original state. The translation of *Namaste* is one of infinite depth. It means:

The divinity in me...salutes the divinity in you.

Here we have an antidote to objectification. Something infinite, immortal, mysterious, loving, and alive abides *in me* and it is from this light that I bow toward that which is infinite, immortal, mysterious, loving, and alive *in you*. What if this was our set-point, our baseline,

Misogyny is absolutely baked into the way we raise children.

the fundamental assumption we had about every single person we encountered? All our reputations precede us: *We're divine.*

When I speak of "divinity" and "spirituality," please know this has nothing to do with texts, codes, or churches. Here's how I loosely define spirituality for myself: understanding that reality constitutes more than we can detect with our five senses; that the source of all creation is also the source of goodness, virtue, and truth; that this source is on our side; and that we can align ourselves with this source and draw upon its power. I call this source "God," but I'm sympathetic to the widespread allergy to the word. Call it what you like. I don't believe God to be a being, by the way. I think of God as more verb than noun. To me, it's energy, it's dynamism, it's flow—and it's good.

Mystics from every tradition testify to the aliveness and sentience of all things, that the natural world is lit up with the flame of divinity. This does and must include us. We're not taught this. In fact, most of what we're taught *opposes* this.

There's an urgency to this moment. We must choose between a world of subjects and a world of objects. To acknowledge the divinity of another, we must first accept our own, which is not nearly as easy as it sounds. Two quotes on this, from Buddhist teacher Jack Kornfield and Jungian analyst and writer Robert Johnson:

> Our belief in a limited and impoverished identity is such a strong habit that without it we are afraid we wouldn't know how to be. If we fully acknowledged our dignity, it could lead to radical life changes. It could ask something huge of us.[5]

> People resist the noble aspects of their shadow more strenuously than they hide the dark sides.... It is more disrupting to find that you have profound nobility of character than to find out you are a bum.[6]

A simple thought experiment proves this: How much easier is it to believe horrible things about ourselves than wonderful things? So many of us carry a kind of unspoken assumption that something is very, very wrong with us, that we're damaged, guilty, and unlovable. Stepping into our divinity—acknowledging and accepting our fundamental nobility—is the ultimate paradigm shift. Kornfield is right. We cannot continue with business as usual after this. Shame cannot coexist with divinity. We cannot serve two masters.

Namaste asks something huge of us: *If the divinity in me recognizes the divinity in you, how could I abuse, debase, violate, or harass?* I would, after all, only be punishing myself.

∾

THERE'S ALWAYS A DANGER in being an on-the-record moralist (see the perennial parade of countless vocal finger-waggers whose closets are bursting with skeletons), but I think it essential to get some more public accounts of men's struggles with their shadows and cultural baggage, while fully acknowledging their actions and the pain they have caused. We are all a product of this broken culture.

Like many men in the last few months, I've been doing a lot of reflection on past behavior: the privilege to which I've been largely blind; microaggressions of which I was unaware; times I've unthinkingly spoken over or minimized the contributions of women; sizing up a woman's sexual currency in a quick, thoughtless, and ravenous glance; waging war on the "feminine" within me and the many insidious ways that spills outward.

It's never easy to look at this stuff, at one's own complicity in oppression (though any "pain" a man might endure in this process of self-reflection is minuscule compared to what women have endured at the hands of bullying and predatory men). I am comforted by this thought: Who we have been is not necessarily who we must become.

St. Gregory of Nyssa offered another beautiful, succinct, and useful definition of sin. *Sin*, he said, *is a refusal to keep growing up.*[7]

This is a growing moment. Growth is painful.

I don't believe hell or heaven to be post-life destinations. I believe they are states of consciousness available here and now. A world of objects is a kind of hell. A world of subjects—divine beings honoring the divinity in the other—is surely heaven. May we point our feet toward this heaven and begin the hard and necessary work of walking there. •

Moral Outrage and the Stickiness of Anger and Disgust

By Joan Halifax

O NE SUMMER EVENING in the 1960s, I stepped out of the building where I lived in New York City and came upon the startling scene of a man yelling at a woman. Suddenly, the man ripped off the radio antenna from an automobile and began to whip the woman with it. Without thinking, I put my body between them and shouted at him to stop. Morally outraged, I had no thought for my own safety. The scene of a man abusing a woman set me afire and I reacted accordingly. As I stood there, heart pounding, the woman hurriedly thanked me and fled the scene. The man threw the antenna onto the street, snarled at me, and walked away.

Moral outrage has been defined as a response of anger and disgust in relation to a perceived moral violation. In that street scene, I was witnessing not only physical violence, but gender violence as well. Fifty years later, the sensation in my body of encountering that violence is still present for me. It was the shock of outrage and revulsion, and nothing could have stopped me from moving between the two of them.

In retrospect, I am pretty sure I was not acting from egoic motivations when I stepped in to stop the violence; I wasn't out to gain the approval of others or boost my self-esteem. I had no time for a self-centered thought—I simply could not slip by this horrifying scene without intervening. What motivated my action was a quick and deep surge of moral outrage, combined with compassion.

Over the years, I've witnessed moral outrage manifesting in healthy and unhealthy forms in the worlds of politics, activism, journalism, and medicine, and in my own personal experience. Attempting to dig below the surface, I've seen that moral outrage, like pathological altruism, can sometimes reflect an unacknowledged need to be perceived as a "good" person. We may believe that our superior moral stance makes us appear more trustworthy and honorable in the eyes of others. Our righteous indignation can give us a lot of ego satisfaction and may relieve us of guilt about our own culpability: "We are right, others are wrong; we are morally superior, others are morally corrupt."

The social critic Rebecca Solnit further unmasks the self-serving dimension of moral outrage in her essay in *The Guardian*: "We Could Be Heroes: An Election-Year Letter." She notes that those on the far left often engage in "recreational bitterness," turning moral outrage into a competitive sport by criticizing everything that happens in electoral politics—even news items that most liberals consider positive. Solnit notes that this stance does not advance any causes and actually undermines alliance-building.[1] Ultimately, I wonder how much recreational bitterness played into the outcome of the 2016 US election by widening the divide between liberals and the far left.

To preserve our integrity, we must speak truth to power.

However, when moral outrage is self-serving ... it can be addictive and divisive.

Recreational bitterness and other forms of moral outrage can be contagious, addictive, and ungrounding, and they can make us sick. A small dose can get us going. Binging on it will do us in, and that's what our adversaries want. When we are angry and emotionally over-aroused, we begin to lose our balance and ability to see things clearly, and we are prone to falling over the edge into moral suffering.

However, many of us feel that we violate our own integrity if we don't hold people accountable for the harm they cause others. In the face of moral violations, we cannot be bystanders or protect ourselves through denial. To preserve our integrity, we must speak truth to power. This is what I call "principled moral outrage."

An important quality of moral outrage is that it involves feelings of revulsion in response to a perceived breach of ethics. Interestingly, social psychologists have studied the effect of disgust on moral discernment. In one study, when jurors in mock trials were exposed to a disgusting smell, they meted out harsher sentences against the defendant. Disgust seemed to amplify their experience of moral outrage, leading to stricter judgments.[2] Another study found that people who tend toward stronger feelings of disgust find people in their in-group more attractive and have more negative attitudes toward people in out-groups.[3] This might be a reason why moral outrage can be so polarizing—it widens the divide between self and other.

Internally, we may have conflicting responses to our own moral outrage. Whereas anger can excite aggression, disgust can produce withdrawal—which can mean hiding within our in-group and objectifying and avoiding the out-group. Martha Nussbaum, an ethicist and jurist, uses the phrase "the politics of disgust" to critique laws that discriminate against the LGBT community on the basis of disgust, such as bans on same-sex marriage and anti-transgender "bathroom bills."[4] She notes that such politics support bigotry, intolerance, and oppression.

As the ethicist Dr. Cynda Rushton writes,

> Moral outrage can become the glue that holds a group together in a sense of solidarity against those who threaten their personal or professional identities, values, beliefs, or integrity. The sense of moral outrage can become contagious and, if unexamined, can exacerbate differences and fuel separation rather than connection and cooperation.[5]

Rational thinking plays an important role, of course, but often a subordinate one. "What makes moral thinking moral thinking is the function that it plays in society, not the mechanical processes that are taking place in the brain," says Harvard psychology professor Joshua Greene.[6]

In some ways, outrage is a justifiable response to an action that is morally transgressive, but even less serious moral issues, like mismanagement of an institution, can cause us anger, disgust, and principled moral outrage. When moral outrage is episodic and regulated, it can be a useful instigator of ethical action. There is plenty about which to be outraged in the world and our anger can give us the energy we need to confront injustice. Strong emotions can help us recognize an immoral situation and can motivate us to intervene, take a stand, even risk our lives to benefit others.

However, when moral outrage is self-serving, chronic, and unregulated—when it becomes the very lens through which we view the world—it can be addictive and divisive. Shaming, blaming, and self-righteousness also put us in a superior power position, which can feel satisfying in the short term but isolates us from others in the long term. Constant over-arousal can also have serious effects on the body, mind, and spirit—from ulcers to depression and everything in between. It can also can have serious effects on how others perceive us.

In the final analysis, I have learned that moral outrage can have beneficial or harmful consequences not only for ourselves, but for our relationships and even our society. Our discernment, insight into our intentions, and our ability to regulate our emotions are what make the difference as to whether or not moral outrage serves us and others.   •

Excerpted and adapted, by permission of the author, from Standing at the Edge: Finding Freedom Where Fear and Courage Meet *by Joan Halifax (New York: Flatiron Books, 2018).*

In Defense of Anger:

The Creative Extremism of Justice and the Prophetic Call for Change

By Mark S. Burrows

ANGER HAS LONG been considered a "no-go" in the Christian tradition. The classic text, from the letter of James, gives voice to this suspicion: "Let everyone be quick to listen, slow to speak, slow to anger; for your anger does not produce God's righteousness" (James 1:19b–20[1]). Generally, Christians have avoided endorsing anger and joined forces with therapeutic efforts at "anger management"—which, at last check, registers more than twenty million website references. Often enough, of course, anger is disturbing. It unsettles the peace. It threatens the order of society. It raises our blood pressure. It troubles our dreams and keeps us awake at night.

Sometimes anger is not only permissible, but necessary. Set against James' often-salutary warning is the long witness of the prophets, often aligned, as in the Book of Jonah, with divine wrath: "Who knows?

God may relent and change his mind; he may turn from his fierce anger, so that we do not perish" (Jonah 3:9). We find it expressed in the scene of Jesus' "cleansing" of the Temple (e.g., Matthew 21:12–16). It is, in short, a tradition with a venerable heritage, rooted in the ancient Hebrew prophets and carrying through the ages. In our own times, it stoked the fervor of the Civil Rights movement in the 1960s. Here, Dr. Martin Luther King, Jr.'s Letter from a Birmingham Jail comes immediately to mind: a prophetic blast against passivity, complacence, and silence in the larger Christian community in the face of the obscene burden of racial injustice.

What lay at the heart of King's call for non-violent direct action—sit-ins, marches, peaceful demonstrations—was a refusal to be silent, given the violent status quo crushing innocent and vulnerable citizens whose only "offense" was the color of their skin. The situation we still face in the United States is appalling in this regard. Against the pressure of the Black Lives Matter movement, which carries forth this resistance in the public sphere, President Trump continues to make statements and send out messages that can only be understood as racist, bigoted, and violent. Here, the words of the psalmist—now not too many to "tweet" in response—come to mind, giving voice to an ancient tradition of outrage and resistance:

> O LORD, you God of vengeance,
>   you God of vengeance, shine forth!
> Rise up, O judge of the earth;
>   give to the proud what they deserve!
> O LORD, how long shall the wicked,
>   how long shall the wicked exult? (Psalm 94:1–3)

We do well to remember that Dr. King wrote this letter under pressure from many contemporaries, among them Christian leaders from many denominations, who criticized his call for justice as "too much, too soon." They argued, against his call for nonviolent resistance, that such actions would only incite violence and disturb the peace, that his tactics were those of an extremist. The jailed preacher had this to say: "The question is not whether we will be extremists, but what kind of extremists we will be. Will we be extremists for hate or for love? Will we be extremists for the preservation of injustice or for the extension of justice?"[2]

This is a question no less urgent today, despite the more than five decades separating us from his appeal. Will we be extremists for the extension of justice? Will we speak out, in public and in private, against the violation of civil rights for all those who live among us? Will we rebuke the "proud" who stamp on civil rights and ignore injustice in our midst? Will we recognize, with Dr. King, that "injustice anywhere is a threat to justice everywhere," particularly when we see, as he did, that "we are caught in an inescapable network of mutuality, tied in a single garment of destiny. Whatever affects one directly, affects all indirectly"?[3] Will our sense of *oneing*, our commitment to join contemplation with action, move from the private into the public sphere? Will our actions embody our inner convictions in opposing the forces of hate? The hour is late, and the stakes are high. As Dr. King put it, two generations ago, "I had hoped that the white moderate would understand that law and order exist for the purpose of establishing justice and that when they fail in this purpose they become the dangerously structured dams that block the flow of social progress."[4]

A scant generation ago, John Bell and the Wild Goose Resource Group—in solidarity with the Iona Community and its work with the Corrymeela Community of Northern Ireland—published a new hymn entitled "Inspired by Love and Anger." The first verse captures the heart of Dr. King's call to avoid what he called "do-nothingism," to resist "the paralyzing chains of conformity" and join the long, and often extremist, prophetic witness against the violence of racial injustice:

Inspired by love and anger, disturbed by need and pain,
informed of God's own bias, we ask him once again:
"How long must some folk suffer? How long can few folk mind?
How long dare vain self-interest turn prayer and pity blind?"[5]

How long, indeed? Do we dare to sing such songs in our churches? Can we find the courage to live out such a witness in our communities, in solidarity with those who suffer unjustly and face the extremism of injustice?

All of this, of course, is set against the painful realization that our public culture is in a state of deep disrepair. We seem locked in the binaries in which the pundits have taught us to believe: red vs. blue; conservative vs. liberal; rich vs. poor; and, to a distressing extent, black vs. white. We are often passive in the face of what we know is wrong, worried that we might ourselves be subject to verbal attack or outright violence. Our abilities to communicate across such culturally imposed divides seem ineffective at best, a failure occasioned in part by the immediacy of communication in the era of Twitter and Instagram. Gone is the discretion that depends upon measured reflection, examination of conscience, and empathy within the horizon of difference.

The private and the public realms, once rather more clearly delineated, are blurred in all this. When we act on our immediate impulses and respond instantly, as we often do, the time-lapse required for forming moral judgments evaporates. We post our opinions, whether on Facebook or through Twitter, before we have sorted out what might be at stake in a given matter. Tweeting is the most extreme version of this: a medium not, in itself, good or bad, but one that is vulnerable to abuse—often that of publicizing urges and opinions better left out of public discourse altogether. We spew our frustrations and dissatisfactions immediately into the public sphere, often with a callous disregard of others.

In all this, we are like those the poet T. S. Eliot (1888–1965) described as "distracted from distraction by distraction," caught in a predicament he voices in a series of claims untroubled by punctuation:

> Filled with fancies and empty of meaning
> Tumid apathy with no concentration
> Men and bits of paper, whirled by the cold wind
> That blows before and after time.[6]

This seems a vivid portrait of the "Trump Era," in which the nation—and, indeed, the world—has become accustomed to greeting each morning with some new e-blast of unconsidered vitriol, thoughtless derision, or worse. All this has come to constitute a cultural distraction *du jour*, as it were; the poet's words seem prescient in describing the dismal tenor that reigns in the public sphere of our times.

Of course, at the heart of this is anger, though of an unreflective and destructive brand, caught in the old binaries that seem ready to stagnate any attempt at that most elemental virtue needed for the flourishing of the *res publica*: civility. It would be hard to find any legitimate argument to endorse such an anger, which I would describe with that old-fashioned word "derision"—a noun deriving from the

Will we speak out, in public and in private, against the violation of civil rights for all those who live among us?

past participle stem of *deridere*, "to ridicule," itself comprised of the prefix "de," meaning "down" and *ridere*, "to laugh." Derisive anger is the métier of bullies; we see this now acted out in the political arena on a regular basis. It has to do with scorn. When coupled with power, it is the short road to every kind of abuse imagined or enacted upon the vulnerable. It is the enemy of that old-fashioned vision of public life once spoken of as the "commonwealth." It thrives on dualisms.

Rarely has it been as vividly described as in the classic tale, *Alice's Adventures in Wonderland*, an articulate cultural critique of mid-nineteenth-century Victorian mores gone awry. Consider, for example, the awkward encounter Alice has with the Mock Turtle, who introduces himself with the insistence that he "had the best of educations." When Alice presses him on the point, he describes the curriculum of the "regular course" he had taken as having consisted of "Reeling and Writhing, of course, to begin with . . . and then the different branches of Arithmetic—Ambition, Distraction, Uglification, and Derision."[7]

Lewis Carroll—the pseudonym for the Oxford don Charles Lutwidge Dodgson (1832–1898)—meant this as a biting satire directed at the smug, self-satisfied culture of his day. It seems, though, to have lost nothing of its poignancy as a mirror of what can go wrong in any society, and has in our own. Something about the sequence—an obvious play on "addition, subtraction, multiplication, and division"—is important: What begins in ambition and is clouded by distraction leads to the demise implied by "uglification" and derision. At the heart of the latter is some mix of anger and fear—again, the stuff that keeps bullies at their work in threating the vulnerable.

There are, of course, other sorts of anger, including that of righteous or prophetic indignation. Here, a clue: If we imagine the opposite of this kind of anger, we do well to think beyond the cliché of "being nice"

Anger, in its noble form, will arise as a creative passion, one intent on building the wholeness of justice among the fragments of disobedience.

and toward complacence, an acquiescence to what is unjust and wrong in our world—and, perhaps, in our own lives. In this sense, the anger that rises as indignation against oppression is a noble form, since it has to do with a resistance against lies in every form, including those rooted in derision, ridicule, and contempt. It is a witness borne of a vision—even when this must be an extremist vision—that opposes polarities and refuses what Dr. King called "the dark clouds of racial prejudice [which, he hoped, would] soon pass away and the deep fog of misunderstanding [that must] be lifted from our fear-drenched communities."[8] These were strong words in 1963. They sting now, with the impatience that has gathered over the last fifty years.

In this noble form, such an anger gives voice to Dr. King's call to recognize each person, regardless of race or nationality, religion or sexual orientation, as belonging to the "whole" of God's reign of justice. It claims the "new creation" promised by the gospel, insisting that this promise is for a "new earth" along with a "new heaven" (see Revelation 21:1–2). It prays and works for the coming of God's kingdom, "on earth as it is in heaven" (Matthew 6:10b). It stands against bigotries of every sort, because they demean the image of God that marks each human being. It stands with the prophet who calls for "justice [to] roll down like waters, and righteousness like an ever-flowing stream" (Amos 5:24). Or, to mix metaphors, it will attempt to answer the psalmist's desperate call—"How long shall the wicked exult" (Psalm 94:3b)—by heeding, with courage, the German-Jewish poet Hilde Domin's "appeal," in a poem of the same name:

Don't go forth as an extinguisher
Don't go forth as an extinguisher
Don't go forth as an extinguisher
into the extinguishing

Burn
Burn
We are torches my brother
We are stars
We are combustible
Rising up
or we've not ever
been[9]

At its core, such an anger, in its noble form, will arise as a creative passion, one intent on building the wholeness of justice among the fragments of disobedience. It is one courageous enough to see that action must join prayer if the latter is to be legitimate. It stands on the side of all who oppose the "uglification" of injustice. It refuses derision, but also resists the lure of "do-nothingism" and "say-nothingism." It stands with these prophets who claimed the truth of justice over the righteousness of truth. And, ultimately, it will turn from complacence, silence, and inaction, seeking to give voice and outward form to an extremism worthy of the gospel heard in the prophets' alternative orthodoxy. •

Arthritis of the Spirit

By Barbara Brown Taylor

Then Peter came and said to him, "Lord, if another member of the church sins against me, how often should I forgive? As many as seven times?" Jesus said to him, "Not seven times, but, I tell you, seventy-seven times."
                                                    —Matthew 18:21–22

IN CASE YOU have not noticed, Christianity is a religion in which the sinners have all the advantages. They can step on your feet fifty times and you are supposed to keep smiling. They can talk bad about you every time you leave the room and it is your job to excuse them with no thought of getting even. The burden is on you, because you have been forgiven yourself, and God expects you to do unto others as God has done unto you.

This is not a bad motivation for learning how to forgive. If God is willing to stay with me in spite of my meanness, my weakness, my stubborn self-righteousness, then who am I to hold those same things against someone else? Better I should confess my own sins than keep track of yours, only it is hard to stay focused on my shortcomings. I would so much rather stay focused on yours, especially when they are hurtful to me.

Staying angry with you is how I protect myself from you. Refusing to forgive you is not only how I punish you; it is also how I keep you from getting close enough to hurt me again, and nine times out of ten it works, only there is a serious side effect. It is called bitterness, and it can do terrible things to the human body and soul.

A while back, I stopped at a gift shop to buy a couple of wedding presents, some nice brass picture frames, which I asked the clerk to wrap. "Well, who are they for?" she snarled. "Are you going to tell me or am I supposed to guess?" I looked at her then for the first time and saw a thickset woman whose brow was all bunched up over two hard, cold eyes. Her mouth turned down at the sides like she had just tasted something rancid and she had both her hands planted on the glass counter, leaning against it with such malice that I thought she might push it over on me if I irritated her any further.

Generally speaking, I get mad when someone comes at me like that, but this time I just got scared, because I could see what her anger had done to her and I wanted to get away from it before it did something similar to me. Actually, it was something stronger than plain anger that had twisted that woman's face. All by itself, anger is not that damaging. It is not much more than that quick rush of adrenaline you feel when you are being threatened. It tells you that something you hold dear is in danger—your property, your beliefs, your physical safety. I think of anger as a kind of flashing yellow light. "Caution," it says, "something is at risk here. Slow down and see if you can figure out what it is."

When I do slow down, I can usually learn something from my anger, and if I am lucky I can use the energy of it to push for change in myself or in my relationships with others. Often I can see my own part in what I am angry about, and that helps, because if I had a hand in it then I can concentrate on getting my hand back out of it again instead of spinning my wheels in blame. I can, in other words, figure out what my anger has to teach me and then let it go, but when my anger goes on and on without my learning or changing anything then it is not plain anger anymore. It has become bitterness instead. It has become resentment, which a friend of mine calls "arthritis of the spirit."

So, there is another motivation for learning how to forgive—not only because we owe it to God but because we owe it to ourselves.

Because resentment deforms us. Because unforgiveness is a boomerang. We use it to protect ourselves—to hurt back before we can be hurt again—but it has a sinister way of circling right back at us so that we become the victims of our own ill will.

One summer *The New York Times Book Review* ran a series on the deadly sins. Joyce Carol Oates wrote on despair, Gore Vidal wrote on pride, and John Updike, of all people, wrote on lust. Mary Gordon's essay on anger was a real beauty, chiefly because she was willing to admit she knew a lot about it. One hot August afternoon, she wrote, she was in the kitchen preparing dinner for ten. Although the house was full of people, no one offered to help her chop, stir, or set the table. She was stewing in her own juices, she said, when her two small children and her seventy-eight-year-old mother insisted that she stop what she was doing and take them swimming.

They positioned themselves in the car, she said, leaning on the horn and shouting her name out the window so all the neighbors could hear them, loudly reminding her that she had promised to take them to the pond. That, Gordon said, was when she lost it. She flew outside and jumped on the hood of the car. She pounded on the windshield. She told her children and her mother that she was never, ever going to take any of them anywhere and none of them was ever going to have one friend in any house of hers until the hour of their death—which, she said, she hoped was soon.

Then the frightening thing happened. "I became a huge bird," she said. "A carrion crow. My legs became hard stalks, my eyes were sharp and vicious. I developed a murderous beak. Greasy black feathers took the place of arms. I flapped and flapped. I blotted out the sun's light

It is scary...to trade in your pride and your power on the off-chance that you may discover something more valuable than either of them.

with my flapping." Even after she had been forced off the hood of the car, she said, it took her a while to come back to herself and when she did she was appalled, because she realized she had genuinely frightened her children. Her son said to her, "I was scared because I didn't know who you were."

"Sin makes the sinner unrecognizable," Gordon concluded, and the only antidote to it is forgiveness, but the problem is that anger is so exciting, so enlivening, that forgiveness can feel like a limp surrender. If you have ever cherished a resentment, you know how right it can make you feel to have someone in the world whom you believe is all wrong. You may not be up to admitting it yet, but one of the great benefits of having an enemy is that you get to look good by comparison. It also helps to have someone to blame for why your life is not turning out the way it was supposed to.

On National Public Radio I once heard Linda Wertheimer talking to a correspondent in the Middle East about the amazing things that were happening there between Israelis and Palestinians. That seems like a long time ago now. "How are people reacting?" she asked him then. "After all, losing an enemy is as upsetting as losing a friend." I hadn't thought about it that way before, but she was right. When you allow your enemy to stop being your enemy, all the rules change. Nobody knows how to act anymore, because forgiveness is an act of transformation. It does not offer the adrenaline rush of anger, nor the feeling of power that comes from a well-established resentment. It is a quiet revolution, as easy to miss as a fist uncurling to become an open hand, but it changes people in ways that anger only wishes it could.

So why don't we do it more often? Because it is scary, to lay down your arms like that, to trade in your pride and your power on the off-chance that you may discover something more valuable than either of them. "To forgive," Gordon wrote, "is to give up the exhilaration of one's own unassailable rightness." And there is loss in that, only it is the loss of an illusion, and what is gained is unmistakably real: the chance to live again, free from the bitterness that draws the sweetness from our lives, that gives us scary faces and turns us into carrion crows who blot out the sun with our flapping. No one else does this to us. We do it to ourselves, but we do not have to.

We are being forgiven every day of our lives. We are being set free by someone who has arranged things so that *we* have all the advantages. We have choices. We have will. And we have an advocate, who seems to know that we need lots of practice at this forgiveness business. How often should we forgive? Will seven times take care of it? "Not seven times," Jesus said, "but, I tell you, seventy-seven times." This is no chore. This is a promise, because forgiveness is the way of life. It is God's cure for the deformity our resentments cause us. It is how we discover our true shape, and every time we do it we get to be a little more alive. What God knows and we don't yet is that once we get the hang of it, seventy times seven won't be enough, not to mention seventy-seven. We'll be so carried away that we'll hope the forgiveness never ends. •

The Role of Anger in Spiritual Work

By Russ Hudson

I N T H E *Star Wars* series, Master Yoda warns his apprentice, Luke Skywalker, about the dangers of anger and aggression, describing them as gateways to the Dark Side of the Force. *Star Wars* is certainly not the first human expression to show anger as evil and as directly rooted in evil. While some people may be more comfortable expressing anger than others, it is certainly rare to find people who are completely comfortable with anger, be it their own or others'. Rarer still are people who are skillful in navigating this entirely unavoidable human emotion. Our fears and misunderstandings around anger are deep-rooted, understandable, and relatively normal, but they do make it much more difficult to walk the spiritual journey with steadiness and clarity.

In the Christian scriptures, we *seem* to get mixed messages about this, but I suggest that the New Testament is telling us about *two qualities* of anger. In Matthew 5:22, Jesus seems to lay out very directly that expressing anger and name-calling are sinful. Things get a little clearer in Ephesians 4:26 (NIV), when Paul says not to "let the sun go down while you are still angry." Here, I would suggest that Paul is saying *do not hold on to your anger*. This is easier said than done. What makes it possible to let our anger flow without holding onto it?

We might say that there is awake, intelligent anger that is a response to a wrongful situation, and there is destructive anger that we are warned against in the scriptures. While we are instructed about the negative effects of anger as reaction, we also see examples where anger is creative and positive. Indeed, Jesus seems to have displayed powerful anger on several occasions—the fig tree and the moneylenders in the temple immediately come to mind. The parable of the wedding banquet and the king in Matthew 22:1–14 also suggests that anger can be an appropriate response. If we grasp this, we naturally want to know how to tell the difference between positive, creative anger and destructive, negative anger.

I would suggest that anger that is held in presence, with awareness and grounding, is creative and helpful. It is quite possible to be angry at someone and love them at the same time. For me, presence is a grace offered in each moment. It allows whatever I am feeling to be transmuted into something useful, for myself, for the situation I may be in, and perhaps for some greater good. When I meet anger with sensation and breath, with a heart of sensitivity and kindness, and with a mind that is open and receptive, the anger is transformed into a powerful force that can be extremely helpful in my life. How do we do this?

> I have learnt through bitter experience the one supreme lesson to conserve my anger, and as heat conserved is transmuted into energy, even so, our anger controlled can be transmuted into a power which can move the world.
> —Mahatma Gandhi

LEARNING TO REMEMBER the grace of presence is already a huge step. For me, *most* of my spiritual journey has been about learning how to be present and, from that grounding in presence, learning how to allow love to be what moves me. Learning to be present to life with awareness and kindness, as it unfolds, is one of the most glorious challenges we will ever undertake. It seems so

The long-term effects of avoiding anger are every bit as corrosive as acting it out.

easy. What could be hard about it? But if we are sincere and persistent in our efforts, we will see that we cannot be present merely through our own intentions. We cannot be present any time we decide to do so. This is shocking and humbling to most of us, and we gradually realize that presence is not an action we take—it is more a recognition of what is. We see that we have been mistaken in some fundamental ways about what makes our transformation possible. Presence seems to be something *received*, that comes to us through a kind of willingness more than through some forceful effort. We come to understand that our will does not operate quite as we might imagine. There is an element of grace, of something miraculous arising in us which gives us the capacity to be awake to our experience.

This is hard enough when conditions are favorable—when we are relaxed and not particularly stressed about anything. However, when powerful emotions arise, it is generally much more difficult to find a ground in us that can be compassionately awake with what we are feeling. As we begin to be present to anger, we begin to discern in our own experience the difference between those two forms of anger.

In this sense, we naturally come to understand the importance of practices—contemplation, meditation, and prayer—as methods to cultivate in ourselves a capacity to be with larger emotions and bigger triggers in our lives. As I often tell my students, "Practice when it is easy and it will be there for you when it is hard." Most of us eventually learn that we can indeed be awake with our sadness, our joy, our disappointments, and many of our reactions. Anger, on the other hand, often remains a bigger challenge. For most of us, the ability to stay awake when we are angry is a real mark of our steadfastness in practice as well as a mark of burgeoning spiritual maturity.

This does not imply that doing our spiritual work means we do not get angry! In fact, I have yet to see a human being who has truly transcended the emotion of anger. There are several examples of Jesus and the prophets displaying righteous anger about injustices and corruptions. So, clearly, we are not being asked to transcend anger, and I am doubtful that we really could do so. A more realistic and grounded spirituality invites us to learn to *navigate* our anger with graciousness while, at the same time, drawing benefit from the grounding and empowering energy it can bring. So how do we do this?

First, we need to recognize anger when, and as, it arises. Many of us do not notice our anger until we are acting on it, and sometimes not even then. Some of us are embarrassed about our feelings of anger and ashamed that we would even have such feelings. This can be especially true if we think of ourselves as spiritual or have grown up in more traditionally religious families. Different cultures in the world have widely different rules and comfort levels with the expression of anger. So, it is important that we are honest about our anger. Just allowing this fact of our humanity is a good way to make some space for inner work to occur. "Yes, the cat is out of the bag. I get angry, and more often than I would like to admit!" This kind of sincerity will also help us to see various ways we mask our anger or present it as something other than what it is.

IF WE ARE honest with ourselves when anger arises, we may begin to notice various familiar trains of thought or tensions in the body that we will recognize as being tied to our anger. This is a big development, because we are noticing the sensations and patterns of the anger rather than being *at the mercy* of their effect. We are mining a deeper layer of the soul when we do this. In my own work, I noticed that, when I was angry, my thoughts would become very repetitive, I would develop an acrid taste in my mouth, and my shoulders would become tense. My co-writer, Don Riso, used to observe that, when he was angry, he would squint and have trouble making eye contact. We learned that it is extremely helpful to be mindful of our own patterns in order to change our fundamental relationship with our anger.

When we are present with our anger, we will notice some amazing things about it. Many of us are surprised to find that we feel more alive when we can be present to the sensation of anger. We feel more energized in our limbs and more connected with the vital energies of the body. Our breathing is released and deeper. However, the reverse is also true: When we are stuck in a pattern of resisting anger, we find it much harder to be with any other life energies. We can begin to lose our vitality because so much life force is needed to suppress what we are feeling.

Further, connecting to the sensation of anger gives us more confidence to speak up or act as needed. It can give us courage to do what we have been afraid to do and to take action when we have been procrastinating. It can connect us with a sense of *righteousness*: doing what God asks us to do, even through our own hesitation, resistance, and fear. When the feeling of vital energy comes together with this natural confidence, it brings a very distinct sense of connection with reality and with life. This sense is in great distinction from being *self-righteous*, which is a way of *not* being honest with ourselves about our anger. Self-righteousness tends to cut us off from the sense of connection and vitality.

Most people are also quite surprised to discover that, when we are present with anger, it lasts only a few seconds—perhaps the duration of two or three breaths. It arises and fills our limbs and belly with feelings of heat and energy and the sense of empowerment. It is our denial and suppression of anger that causes it to stay in us for much longer periods of time—ricocheting around in our nervous system until we are ready to finally feel it. For some of us, it remains as a simmering resentment and negativity; for others, it leaves us with a quick temper; for still others, it is so suppressed that it lives in our tissues, slowly poisoning our bodies with repressed, unresolved energies. When we are awake with the actual sensation of anger, it shows up just long enough to help us and is then dissolved into the next feeling or state.

In my own inner work, I make a distinction between *conscious* or *necessary* anger and *unconscious* or *unnecessary* anger. The former is more along the lines of what we have been exploring and is a response to an injustice or violation that is occurring now, either within me or around me. The latter is a form of unconscious *frustration* stemming from unresolved issues I am bringing to a situation. Something from the past is being overlaid on my experience. I might, for example, be

There is awake, intelligent anger that is a response to a wrongful situation, and there is destructive anger that we are warned against in the scriptures.

frustrated because someone is not being what I need them to be for me. They may not be seeing something in me that I want them to see, or they might be acting in a way incompatible with my own unconscious plans for them. They may be having the audacity to view a situation differently than the way I want them to see it. Most anger is this latter kind—an unconscious response of frustration from the past.

What is interesting about both kinds of anger is that they are *unchosen*. No one *decides* when and how they will be angry or what will trigger their anger. As seekers of truth and the deeper ways of the heart, we learn to recognize anger when it arises and to be present with it. This changes everything. When the anger is a real response to a real situation, being awake to it gives us a grounding that allows us to take a stand and speak our truth as needed. When anger is a pattern arising from our past, the grace of presence allows us to see the pattern for what it is and opens our heart to a wide variety of other emotions and energies which are likely also part of the experience. We might become aware of sadness, or insecurity, or recognize that we want something. Thus, it is always a victory when we can be present to our anger, whatever its source may be.

I N THE ENNEAGRAM system, anger plays a key role in the structures of the nine type patterns and is the basis of one of the three triads—what some call "the anger triad"—which includes types Eight, Nine, and One. I would not say that these Enneagram points are any angrier than the others, but the way they deal with anger is central to their personality structures. As we have seen, when we are present with our anger, it moves through us quickly and can be very useful. When we are not, we need to do *something* with it—not having anger is not an option!

The Eight, Nine, and One represent what we do with anger when we do not know how to remain present and awake with it. In other words, each of us is offered three "menu choices" for what to do with our anger if we are not willing to feel it. All human beings, regardless of their dominant Enneagram type, will tend to prefer one of these methods of dealing with their anger.

Point Eight is the pattern of "acting out" our anger rather than feeling it: Discharging its energy by raising our voice or by behaving in a more aggressive or forceful manner. When we act out our anger, we do not really experience it, so we do not actually get rid of it. We lose our temper and not only retain the emotional chemicals in our bodies, but also often damage our relationships or our standing in situations in the process. Unchecked, this method of dealing with anger can become abusive and harmful to others as well.

Many people think that experiencing anger *is* acting it out. There were even therapies in the 1970s that sought to get people in touch with their anger by acting it out. However, there is a world of difference between being present with the energy of anger in our body and letting that anger provoke us to destructive behaviors. Some of us are frightened of accessing our anger precisely because we think that doing so means acting it out. Perhaps we have seen others do that in our youth and want no part of it. This often leads to an avoidance and denial of anger, an ineffective solution.

Point Nine represents the denial of anger: "I am not an angry person. Spiritual people do not get angry." This pattern tends to fear anger, in self or in others, and values patience, gentleness, and ease. While these are, of course, important human values, they do not work well as a hedge *against* anger. When we run this pattern, we tend to *leave ourselves* whenever anger arises. In psychological language, this is called dissociation and, while it can circumvent the expression of anger in the short term, it often leads to feelings of powerlessness, unimportance, and submerged resentment. When we employ this defense, we collapse in the face of anger, although we may rationalize this as "taking the higher road." At such times, we may not realize how much we are coming across as judgmental and superior. While we might live this way for a while, the anger eventually comes up. Despite our rationalizations and avoidances, the anger remains, sometimes working its way into the tissues and cells of the body and causing illnesses, and sometimes building under the surface until some small and relatively insignificant event triggers an aggressive outburst.

It has been my privilege to work with a group called the Enneagram Prison Project, which has provided me with the opportunity to help incarcerated men and women understand what got them into trouble and recognize the good qualities in themselves. It surprised me how many people—who are in prison for violent acts, even murder—were the ones who employed the avoidance of anger. In addition, many worked hard to "stay positive" and simply went into a rage when life brought up too many triggers and memories of their own painful histories. I mention this because this method of dealing with

There is a world of difference between being present with the energy of anger in our body and letting that anger provoke us to destructive behaviors.

anger is often easily justified and defended in spiritual circles. Yet, in my experience, the long-term effects of avoiding anger are every bit as corrosive as acting it out.

The third menu choice is associated with point One and is based in trying to contain our anger—to repress it and hold it inside. This is different from denying it and dissociating from the experience of it. When we repress anger, we get more tense and rigid. We breathe shallowly and we tend to express our anger indirectly, in sarcasm, put-downs, and terse impatience. In this pattern, we may also feel shame about our anger and therefore seek a good reason for it. While our outrage may indeed be justified, our lack of presence with the anger causes it to leak out in our communications with others, even when we are doing our best to be steady and rational. People feel the anger and react to it, often ignoring good points we may be making. When we use this approach, people feel disrespected. Once others react to us, often rejecting our advice or suggestions, we become even more angry and tense, while still attempting to convince ourselves we are only being sensible and rational.

From the Enneagram perspective, it is crucial to learn to recognize these patterns for dealing with anger *while they are occurring*. If we can do so, bringing presence in body, heart, and mind, we will then contact the sensation of the actual energy of anger. We see through the repetitive thoughts around it. Instead of tensing our bodies and our breath, we relax into this energy and allow the grace of awareness to transmute the anger into something usable—the good, creative anger that is necessary for addressing the difficulties of this world. This becomes another reminder and inspiration for prayer and meditation, forming a real bridge between action and contemplation. Our actions are now a response rather than a reaction and our anger may indeed be present, but no longer causes us to forget the constant presence of love.   •

The Second Sacred Gate:

Grief, Anger, and Transformation

By Mirabai Starr

G RIEF IS HOLY ground. When someone we love dies, we are granted access to a numinous landscape that, like the Isle of Mont Saint-Michel, can only be reached during the low tide of deep sorrow.

Contemporary Western society tries to convince us that death is a failure and grief is a pathological condition, but our souls know better. When we come face-to-face with the mystery of death (or the mystery of birth), we are likely to experience a Moses-like urge to take off our sandals and press our faces into the dust. Even as our hearts are broken by loss, they are broken open by love.

FIVE FEATURES OF THE GRIEF LANDSCAPE

IN THE 1960S, Swiss psychiatrist and pioneer of the conscious dying movement, Elizabeth Kübler-Ross (1926–2004), came up with a heuristic device to describe certain universal features of the grief journey that many bereaved people encounter. Never intended as a fixed map for navigating the wilderness of grief, Kübler-Ross' model of "stages" has rescued millions of mourners from erroneously concluding that they were going crazy as they careened through each of these painful emotional states: denial, anger, bargaining, depression, and acceptance, often circling back, again and again. (Importantly, Kübler-Ross initially conceived of these categories as they applied to terminally ill patients coming to grips with their own impending death, then found that they reflected the grief process even more precisely.)

As someone who has had ample opportunity to abide in the sacred space of grieving (having lost a daughter, a brother, a lover, my dad, and many close friends), I am interested in how each of these landmarks, or sacred gates, serve as thresholds to be honored, rather than simply difficult emotions to be endured and transcended. In other words, instead of approaching death as a problem to be solved (an endeavor pre-programmed for failure), I try to show up for the fully, deeply, profoundly human and holy experience of loss. I do not, of course, always succeed in making myself available for such an encounter. Like any contemplative practice, saying yes to the blessing of what is—no matter how fearsome—requires that we continually renew our intention, cultivating the courage and tenderness such a naked state of being demands.

THE STIGMA

MOST OF US are conditioned to be ashamed of our personal anger. It's okay if we are angry in the face of injustice. A favorite motto of activists, after all, is, "If you're not outraged, you're not paying attention." But outrage is different from rage. When anger flares like a thunderbolt, it can take down the whole forest—incinerating our relationships and requiring major cleanup. No wonder we fear getting angry. It's not comfortable to lose control.

When we experience the death of someone close to us, however, it becomes painfully obvious that we are not in control of the universe. This can trigger a terrifying sensation of free-fall, as if we were hurtling through space without any ground in sight. Our emotions may be wildly unfamiliar. We wonder, "Who is this woman I've become, who suddenly cannot bear the sound of her best friend's chewing?" or "What happened to the man I used to be, who would rather spontaneously combust than yell at his kids?"

Yet bereaved people are likely to find themselves, at times, spilling over with anger, which adds to the generalized pain in which they are already living. It is at the heart of this vulnerability that we can find the passageway to the center of our own experience and recognize the divine presence filling the horizons of our heart. This invites a counterintuitive response. The challenge is to defy cultural expectations—that we must either justify or apologize for feeling anger in the face of great loss—and instead allow ourselves to fully feel it, become curious about it, and bless it as a messenger of love.

SACRALIZING ANGER

I F GRIEF IS a natural response to loss (and I believe it is; don't you?), then anger, as a common attribute of grief, is also natural. The power of our anger often correlates with the depth of our love. Anger takes many forms on the grief journey. Sometimes it manifests as a low-level irritability and other times as roaring fire, often unleashing itself on inappropriate targets. Sometimes it is directed at an individual we deem responsible for our loss: "How could that stupid doctor have overlooked the tumor?" or "The drunk driver who ran over my brother should be locked up for the rest of his life!" or "How could she have killed herself, leaving behind three small children?"

Sometimes the anger is directed at God: "What kind of God could allow such suffering?" or "I was taught to believe God loved me. Apparently, that was wrong." or "Why would God send angels to protect that woman's teenagers and let mine die in a car crash?" While it is tempting to reduce this experience to a crisis of faith, such an easy explanation might obscure the rich spiritual transformation that is unfolding, as John of the Cross (1542–1591) might say, in the darkness of our own souls. Everything we thought we knew feels

The power of our anger often correlates with the depth of our love.

like it is unraveling and we have nowhere to turn but into the center of radical unknowing. Grief shatters our foundation and triggers a wholesale reorientation of meaning. Before we rush off to reconfigure the shards, we may choose to sit in the wreckage and allow ourselves to simply be broken.

From that place of devastation, we come face-to-face with our own groundlessness. We also get to see the extreme poverty of our previous conception of God. The box in which we had always confined the sacred has been demolished by the violence of our loss. The God we fabricated (with the help of society, our family, the church) has fled. No wonder we feel abandoned. No wonder we are angry. But that god was not *the* God. Our souls know that now. We recognize the illusion and begin to suspect that we have been tilting at windmills when we rail against God for forsaking us. Grief is an opportunity to reclaim an authentic connection with Mystery.

Anger often follows denial in the trajectory of grief. Denial doesn't mean we are delusional and believe that what happened didn't happen. Rather, in the wake of fresh loss, our brains are flooded with chemicals designed to numb us from a direct confrontation with the painful facts, allowing our psyche to gradually integrate the new reality. We may enter a kind of dreamlike state in which we function as automatons, making it through the day but not fully connected with our life.

But this initial phase isn't all about shutting down. It can also be a space of grace. When we endure a shattering loss, we may at first sense the presence of unseen beings rushing in to hold us. Because we are culturally conditioned to see death as the enemy, we may keep this spiritual gift to ourselves, afraid no one would understand. We don't understand it ourselves, and yet it sustains us. Another blessing of this initial phase of the grief journey is that a death is often the occasion for community to gather. We may never know how much we are loved and supported until someone close to us dies and friends and acquaintances drop everything to ease our burden.

However, denial eventually passes. The truth of our loss begins to settle on our hearts and we may feel we cannot bear it. We lash out, often at the most convenient and least deserving targets, and then feel terrible about ourselves. Moreover, the people who had recently seemed so eager to help us through have returned to their own lives and we are left in the desert of our anguish. We can't help but resent their growing unavailability, even as, on a rational level, we understand that this is as it should be.

Like a physical desert, this seemingly barren space teems with spiritual energy. God lives here, hidden under every stone, flaming from the harsh sun, concealed by the crescent moon.

ANGER AS ENERGY

WHEN WE GET into a head-on collision with loss, it is as if a vital part of our souls is split off from our bodies. We abide in this fragmented state for a time, disconnected from our own life force and the vitality of the universe. Anger can jumpstart our spiritual battery. We may not choose to feel anger (as opposed to contentment, say, or romantic desire), but it's better than feeling nothing. Anger reminds us that, for better or worse, we are still alive.

This maps beautifully onto the intersection between contemplative life and social and environmental action. Apathy is complicity. When we allow ourselves to go to sleep while human rights are being violated and Mother Earth is being desecrated, we cease to be fully alive, fully human. Anger is a natural response when we let the pain of the world into our hearts. It is not the only appropriate response, of course. However, when we can welcome the fire of the Prophets into our own lives, we tap into the true nature of righteousness and draw the vigor necessary to step up in service to that which is greater than ourselves. We remember our essential interconnectedness with all that is and we are motivated to act on the impulse to protect the web of inter-being with all our might.

Personal and planetary grief are inextricable. Our encounter with the manifold losses that characterize the human experience can till the soil of our hearts so that we are more available to the suffering of other beings and the earth we share. When we have been broken, we recognize the brokenness around us and compassion naturally grows. Sorrow can be paralyzing at first, but compassion, which can sometimes take the form of anger, is a wellspring that offers infinite sustenance. As long as we resist the urge to believe everything we think and train ourselves to be as fully present with reality as we can be, anger becomes another one of the ways the Holy expresses its love, through us, for all that is. •

Anger, Contemplation, and Action

By Brian D. McLaren

Y OU BET I'm angry.

It might not show, because I'm a pretty chill person.

But, just beneath the surface, it's there. Not seething, but burning: burning *hot*. And I'm not proud of it.

But I'm not ashamed of it, either. I'm learning to acknowledge it for what it is.

Why am I angry?

Let's start with the planet. We know that our civilization runs on fossil fuels, and we know that burning these fuels pumps carbon into the atmosphere, and we know this carbon acts like a blanket, holding in heat. We know all this. But because of greedy corporate elites and their bought-and-paid-for politicians, nothing changes. In fact, lately, we have made almost every stupid decision possible.

And it's not just carbon in the air. Our oceans are being acidified and coral reefs are dying. There are huge dead zones in our oceans, along with whirling vortexes of plastic trash. Across the world, our fisheries are collapsing due to overfishing. On land, we're depleting vital aquifers that take tens of thousands of years to recharge. We're squandering soil, we're ravaging forests, and we're driving species to extinction. Why? To turn long-term, irreplaceable assets—which belong as much to future, unborn generations as to this born and greedy one—into short-term cash for a few avaricious families at the top of the global economic pyramid.

We haven't even begun to talk about racism, America's original sin, or the white slaveholder theology that supports it, theology that's rooted deep in so-called Christian orthodoxy and which has, so far at least, hardly been named, much less rooted out. I'm really angry about racism and the white Christian nationalism cocktail on which so many of my neighbors are getting drunk.

Nor have we stirred up the hornets' nest of the global weapons trade and the peculiar obsession of Americans with guns, by which we seek safety through the proliferation of danger and threat. I don't even want to mention our president and all that he represents.

I think about things I love…birds, trees, wetlands, forested mountains, coral reefs, my grandchildren…and I see the bulldozers and smokestacks and tanks on the horizon.

And so, because I love, I am angry. Really angry.

And if you're not angry, I think you should check your pulse, because if your heart beats in love for something, someone, anything… you'll be angry when it's harmed or threatened.

To paraphrase René Descartes (1596–1650): I love; therefore, I'm angry.

The question is what we're going to do with our anger, because Friedrich Nietzsche (1840–1900) was right at least once: "Beware that, when fighting monsters, you yourself do not become a monster."[1] In other words, because I love, I become angry when what I love is threatened. But my anger can lead me, if I am not careful, to become a hateful person. How can I manage or harness anger without being embittered and "monsterified" by it? A good place to start is by seeking to understand it.

ANGER MAKES MOST sense to me through an analogy of pain. What pain is to my body, anger is to my soul, psyche, or inner self. When I put my hand on a hot stove, physical pain reflexes make me react quickly, to address with all due urgency whatever is damaging my fragile tissues. Physical pain must be strong enough to prompt me to action, immediate action, or I will be harmed, even killed.

Similarly, when I or someone I love is in the company of insult, injustice, injury, degradation, or threat, anger awakens. It tells me to change my posture or position; it demands I address the threat. So far, so good—but things get complicated really fast, because anger is tricky.

For example, a friend of mine had an amputation that left him with phantom pain: the feeling that his nonexistent arm was on fire. It was a false sensation, but the pain was all too real. Similarly, we often feel real anger in response to perceived dangers or offenses that, simply put, are no more present than my friend's amputated arm.

In the United States right now, for example, unscrupulous politicians have stirred up vicious resentment against immigrants: "They steal our jobs! They're criminals and rapists!" The truth is that American jobs have been lost largely because of trade policy, automation, and economic recessions, not immigration, and immigrants are statistically less violent and dangerous than people who were born in the US. Even though the stimulus is a phantom, the angry response is real, and that anger can lead people to commit hate crimes, vote for hateful politicians, and pass hateful laws . . . in other words, to become monsters.

So, precisely because our anger is so automatic, so reflexive, it can render us sitting ducks for manipulation by demagogues.

At the core of contemplative practice is the simple realization that we are not our thoughts and reactions.

EVOLUTIONARY BIOLOGISTS TELL us that way back in our vertebrate family tree, our distant ancestors developed five responses to stimuli. Scientists often (jokingly) refer to them as the five Fs:

1. Fight with it!
2. Flee it!
3. Freeze to hide from it!
4. Feed on it!
5. Mate with it!

In highly evolved mammals like us, anger-stimulus usually prompts fight, flight, or freeze responses. If we think the threat is easily defeated, we fight it. If we think it can't be defeated, we flee from it. If we feel it can be neither fled from nor fought, we freeze in place, camouflaging ourselves in hopes that we won't be noticed, the threat will depart, and the anger will dissipate.

Many of us can look back at our lives and see which of these three primary anger responses we prefer.

1. Some of us habitually clench our fists, preparing for a fight. We have a history of angry outbursts, of arguments that we "won" but relationships that we lost.

2. Some of us habitually look for an escape route, preparing for flight. We are conflict avoiders who have a history of evasions, evacuations, and abandonments.

3. Some of us habitually freeze, seeking to keep a low profile until the anger-stimulus passes. We have a history of hiding or stuffing our true feelings, with all the personal and relational consequences of concealment.

At the core of contemplative practice is the simple realization that we are not our thoughts and reactions. Through contemplation, we learn to detach from our thoughts and reactions. To detach is not to deny or suppress. Rather, to detach is to create space between our thoughts and reactions and our truer, deeper self, so our truer, deeper self can observe rather than be controlled by our thoughts and reactions.

Without contemplation, our inner talk in response to, say, a racist joke, might sound like this:

1. A racist joke! I'll expose that idiot's white privilege! He'll never know what hit him! I'll make him pay for his offensive ignorance.

2. A racist joke! How can I get away from this guy? He disgusts me! I'll be sure to avoid him in the future too.

3. A racist joke! Maybe if I don't say anything, he'll think I agree and I won't have to deal with this. I don't want to risk offending him by confronting him. He doesn't need to know how I feel.

With contemplation, instead of getting sucked into fight, flight, or freeze reflexes, our inner dialogue can go something like this:

1. Look at that! I am ready to respond to this guy's insults with my own insults! There goes my fight reflex again. Good thing I don't have to fall into that trap.

2. Look at that! I'm only concerned about my own safety and I'm willing to run away rather than deal with this situation in a healing, constructive way. Thank God I don't have to be controlled by my flight reflex.

3. Look at that! I'm willing to be dishonest and therefore complicit in order to avoid an unpleasant situation. I'm so grateful I have enough distance from my freeze reflex that I don't need to be mastered by it.

This kind of detachment not only saves us from our own reflexes, it also frees us from bondage to our mirror neurons. Psychologists (and mimetic theorists in the tradition of René Girard [1923–2015]) remind us that we tend to mirror the behavior of others. So, if someone speaks to me with kindness, I'll tend to respond in kind, but if they assault me with anger and vitriol, I'll tend to respond in mirrored meanness, unless I have learned to detach from my thoughts and natural reactions. Then my inner dialogue might unfold like this:

Wow! This guy is angry at me. I'll probably feel my adrenaline rise and be tempted to fight fire with fire, but I'm learning to detach from those reactions. So I'll take a deep breath and compose myself and let my angry reaction rise—because it's natural—and then pass, because I am not my thoughts and reactions.

In the split second when anger arises, contemplative practice guides me in letting both my fight/flight/freeze reflexes and my mirror-neuron reactions pass without acting on them. It helps me let one other thing pass as well—my need to judge: "Wow, that guy is a racist! What a jerk!" "Wow, she has a temper problem! She's so immature!" "Wow, he's a bully, and she's a hypocrite, and they're a bunch of blowhards!"

This kind of moralistic judging is the specialty of the dualistic mind. It is highly deceptive in that it renders us morally superior in our own minds, even as it degrades us into proud ("I'm better than they are!"), judgmental (habitually finding fault with others), and hypocritical (critical of others but not myself) persons.

Beyond that, habitual judging is also a first step down a slippery slope of dehumanization. First, we use degrading labels and language to reduce a multidimensional human being into a "bad person"—a racist jerk or hot-tempered baby or lying hypocrite or loudmouthed idiot. Then, as anger simmers, we further demote someone to the status of less than a full human being by calling them a body part—you pick which part. Then, we might use an animal name to further diminish them: jackass, pig, dog, bitch, cockroach. If we let anger take us even further down that slippery road, exclusion or violence can seem like an act of fumigation...cleansing...rather than cruelty. Voilá! In fighting the monster, we have become the monster, and of what atrocities will we now be capable?

In this way, we could say that consistent contemplative practice literally saves lives. But a contemplative mind and heart are not only valuable for what they inhibit. Contemplative practice is also powerful in what it unleashes.

Anger does its work. It prompts us to action, for better or worse.

Having detached from predictable fight/flight/freeze reflexes, mirror reactions, and moralistic judgments, we are free to look for a creative response. Here is where biblical wisdom, ingrained in us through Lectio Divina and related meditative practices, can come to our aid.

> Don't be overcome with evil. Overcome evil with good.
> (see Romans 12:21)

> When someone strikes you on the right cheek, turn the other cheek. (see Luke 6:29)

> Do not return evil to evil to anyone. (see Romans 12:17)

> Bless those who persecute you. Bless, and do not curse.
> (see Romans 12:14)

In each case, we're given alternatives to our natural reactions, alternatives that break us out of fight/flight/freeze, mirroring, and judging. In the split second when we take that long, deep breath, we might breathe out a prayer: "Guide me, Spirit of God!" We might pause to hear if the Spirit inspires us with some non-reactive, non-reflexive response.

It might be a question rather than a judgment: "I'm curious. Were you aware of the racist dimensions of that joke?" Or it might be a confession—an act of vulnerability: "Ouch! I know you meant that to be funny, but that really made me uncomfortable!" Or it might be a request: "Could you do me a favor? In the future, will you avoid jokes like that when I'm around? They make me feel dirty." Or it might be an expression of surprise: "Wow! I always think of you as a kind and fair-minded person, so that joke really seems out of character to me."

Or we might not pause. The truth is, we all too often fall for the reflexive, reactive, judgmental chatter of our monkey minds. We let anger call the shots rather than wisdom and love. It will only be later when our conscience will nag us: "Something's wrong! Your heart isn't healthy. You're simmering in resentment."

And that's a wonderful thing about learning to do our inner work in the context of contemplative practice. Even if we fall into our unhelpful thoughts twenty times, there's always opportunity twenty-one. So smoldering anger sets off our fire alarm and, the next day, we make a phone call. "Hey, friend. I realized late last night that I was angry with you about something. I don't want to be angry with you, so I wanted to clear the air. Would now be OK for a quick conversation?"

Anger does its work. It prompts us to action, for better or worse. With time and practice, we can let the reflexive reactions of fight/flight/freeze, mirroring, and judging pass by like unwanted items on a conveyor belt. Also, with practice, we can make space for creative actions to be prompted by our anger . . . actions that are in tune with the Spirit of love, joy, peace, patience, kindness, gentleness, faithfulness, and self-control (see Galatians 5:22) . . . actions that overcome evil with good and bring healing instead of hate.

So, yes, you bet I'm angry. It's a source of my creativity. It's a vaccination against apathy and complacency. It's a gift that can be abused—or wisely used. Yes, it's a temptation, but it's also a resource and an opportunity, as unavoidable and necessary as pain. It's part of the gift of being human and being alive.   •

lord
give your voice to the silenced
for then rebellion
might grow from their gaze
and grant
that i lend form to this urge
so that i might grasp the tumult of the spray
and the perseverance of the leaves of grass

lord
rip them apart
those membranes between us
made of breath and lies
let me be loud and overbearing in my prayer
so that you wake up and
attend to my desires
for i want to watch your work
without falsity without regard

"Psalm 19" and "Psalm 43" by the Iranian Poet SAID[1]

NOTES

Eficacia De La Paciencia

1 *The Collected Works of St. Teresa of Ávila*, trans. Kieran Kavanaugh and Otilio Rodriguez (Washington, DC: ICS Publications, 1980), III:386.

Contemplating Anger

1 Cornel West, *Race Matters* (New York: Vintage, 1994), 118.

2 Barbara A. Holmes, *Race and the Cosmos: An Invitation to View the World Differently* (New York: T & T Clark, 2002), 15.

3 Lawrence Ware, "Why I'm Comfortable Being an Angry Black Man," *The Root*, November 6, 2016, https://www.theroot.com/why-im-comfortable-being-an-angry-black-man-1790857585.

4 Ibid.

5 Jesse Williams, as cited in Veronica Toney, "Jesse Williams gave one of the most memorable speeches in award show history," *The Washington Post*, June 27, 2016, https://www.washingtonpost.com/news/arts-and-entertainment/wp/2016/06/27/jesse-williams-gave-one-of-the-most-memorable-speeches-in-award-show-history-full-transcript/?utm_term=.0998340aa995.

6 Morgan Winsor and Julia Jacobo, "Pastor Shouts at Governor: 'This Is Black Grief,' After Police Shooting of Minnesota Man," *ABC News*, July 7, 2016, http://abcnews.go.com/US/pastor-challenges-minnesota-gov-put-action-cop-shooting/story?id=40406186.

The Virtue of Anger

1 William Blake, "Never Seek to Tell thy Love," https://www.poetryfoundation.org/poems/43679/never-seek-to-tell-thy-love.

2 Dante Alighieri, *The Divine Comedy*, trans. Henry Wadsworth Longfellow (Boston: Houghton Mifflin, 1895), II:149.

3 Mario Benedetti, *Only in the Meantime*, trans. Harry Morales (Austin: Host Publications, 2006), 17.

4 Elvis Presley, "All Shook Up," *From Memphis to Vegas/From Vegas to Memphis*, RCA Victor, 1969, LP Album.

The Costly Loss of Lament

1 Claus Westermann, *Praise and Lament in the Psalms* (Atlanta: John Knox Press, 1981), and also *The Psalms: Structure, Content and Message* (Minneapolis: Augsburg, 1980).

2 Westermann, *Praise and Lament*, 33, 75, and passim.

3 How that intervention of God happened is unclear. The most formidable hypothesis is that of Hans Joachim Begrich, "Das Priesterliche Tora," *Zeitschrift fur die Alttestamentliche Wissenschaft* 66 (1936), 81–92, reprinted in *Gesammelte Studien zum Alten Testament* (ThB 21; München: Chr. Kaiser Verlag, 1964), 217–310. Begrich proposes that a priestly oracle of salvation was spoken in the midst of the lament which moved the speech from plea to praise. On Begrich's contribution, see Thomas M. Raitt, *A Theology of Exile* (Philadelphia: Fortress, 1977).

4 Westermann, *Praise and Lament*, 27–30.

5 Harvey H. Guthrie, *Theology as Thanksgiving* (New York: Seabury, 1981), 18–19, shrewdly correlates form-critical insights with sociological realities.

6 The relinquishment here accomplished is liturgical, rhetorical, and emotional, but I think it is important to correlate that form of relinquishment to the economic relinquishment urged by Marie Augusta Neale, *A Socio-Theology of Letting Go* (New York: Paulist Press, 1975). I believe the two forms of relinquishment are intimately related to each other. It follows then that the loss of lament as a mode of letting go makes the possibility of economic relinquishment more problematic and sure to be met with resistance.

7 On the reality of social practice related to this Psalm, see my paper, "Psalm 109: Three Times 'Steadfast Love,'" *Word and World* 5^2(1985), 28–46.

8 For this understanding of the social power of speech forms, see Peter L. Berger and Thomas Luckmann, *The Social Construction of Reality* (Garden City, NY: Doubleday, 1966). For this understanding applied specifically to the lament Psalms, see Walter Brueggemann, "The Formfulness of Grief," *Interpretation* 31 (1977), 273–275.

9 A convenient summary of the theory is offered by Charles V. Gerkin, *The Living Human Document* (Nashville: Abingdon, 1984), 82–96. I am grateful to Gerkin for suggesting some lines of my present research.

10 D. W. Winnicott, *The Maturational Processes and the Facilitating Environment* (London: Hogarth, 1965), 145.

11 On the social dimensions of the problem of evil and theodicy, see Peter Berger, Robert Merton, and especially Jon Gunnemann, *The Moral Meaning of Revolution* (New Haven: Yale University Press, 1979).

12 On the relation of God and justice, *theos* and *dikē*, in the Old Testament understanding of theodicy, see Walter Brueggemann, "Theodicy in a Social Dimension," *Journal for the Study of the Old Testament* 33 (1985), 3–25, and *The Message of the Psalms* (Minneapolis: Augsburg, 1984), 168–176.

13 On such boldness in biblical prayer, see Moshe Greenberg, *Biblical Prose Prayer* (Berkeley: University of California Press, 1983), 11–14 and passim.

14 On the cruciality of this cry for the shape of Israel's faith, see James Plastara, *The God of Exodus* (Milwaukee: Bruce Publishing, 1966), 49–59.

15 This emphasis on social evil is a departure from the otherwise splendid statement of James L. Crenshaw, *Theodicy in the Old Testament* (Philadelphia: Fortress, 1983), 1–16. Crenshaw characterizes the issue only with reference to "moral, natural and religious" evil. I believe such a characterization is inadequate because of the great stress in the Old Testament on social justice and injustice.

16 Fascination with "meaning" was especially advanced by Paul Tillich, *Courage to Be* (New Haven: Yale University Press, 1952), 41–42 and passim. In retrospect, Tillich's triad of death, guilt, and meaningfulness, as it applies to the modern period, is uncritically idealist. A more materialist sense of social reality could not settle so readily for the category of "meaning" as the modern agenda.

17 On the function of civility as a mode of social control, see John M. Cuddihy, *The Ordeal of Civility* (New York: Basic Books, 1974) and Norbert Elias, *Power and Civility* (New York: Panthom, 1982).

18 On the rhetorical power of the conjunction, see James Muilenburg, "The Form of Structure of the Covenantal Formulations," *Vetus Testamentum* 9 (1959), 74–79.

19 My analysis was completed before I saw the elegant exposition by Robert Alter, *The Art of Biblical Poetry* (New York: Basic Books, 1985), 67–73. Alter also has seen that the movement of silence and speech is crucial in this Psalm:

On the contrary, the ancient Hebrew literary imagination reverts again and again to a bedrock assumption about the efficacy of speech, cosmogonically demonstrated by the Lord (in Genesis 1) who is emulated by man. In our poem, the speaker's final plea that God hear his cry presupposes the efficacy of speech, the truth-telling power with which language has been used to expose the supplicant's plight. . . . The first two lines present a clear development of intensification of the theme of silence–from a resolution not to offend by speech, to muzzling the mouth, to preserving (in a chain of three consecutive synonyms) absolute muteness. The realized focal point of silence produces inward fire, a state of acute distress that compels a reversal of the initial resolution and issues in speech.

20 Erhard Gerstenberger, "Der klagende Mensch," *Probleme biblischer Theologie*, ed. Hans Walter Wolff (München: Chr. Kaiser Verlag, 1971), 64–72, has shown how the complaint (in contrast to a lament of resignation) is in fact an act of hope.

21 Jose Miranda, *Communism in the Bible* (Maryknoll, NY: Orbis, 1981), 44, has concluded, "It can surely be said that the Psalter presents a struggle of the just against the unjust." His argument is an insistence that *raša'* must not be rendered as a religious category, because it concerns issues of social power and social justice.

22 On the social situation of the sojourner, see Frank Anthony Spina, "Israelites as *gerim*, 'Sojourners,' in Social and Historical Context," *The Word of the Lord Shall Go Forth*, ed. Carol L. Meyers and M. O'Connor (Winona Lake, IL: Eisenbrauns, 1983), 321–335. Not unrelated to that social status, see Spina's more extended study on social rage, "The Concept of Social Rage in the Old Testament and the Ancient Near East" (Unpublished Dissertation, University of Michigan, 1977). This Psalm may be related to social rage around the question of theodicy.

Saluting the Divinity in You

1 See, for example, Richard Rohr, *Adam's Return* (New York: Crossroad, 2004).

2 Terry Pratchett, *Carpe Jugulum* (New York: Harper Torch, 1998), 278.

3 Salma Hayek, "Harvey Weinstein Is My Monster Too," *The New York Times*, December 12, 2017, https://www.nytimes.com/interactive/2017/12/13/opinion/contributors/salma-hayek-harvey-weinstein.html.